A Burmese Journey
and Other Narratives

Travesía por Birmania
y otros relatos

A Burmese Journey
and Other Narratives

Armando Lindner

Travesía por Birmania
y otros relatos

All Bilingual Press
www.allbilingual.com

Published by All Bilingual Press - Seattle, WA

Cover picture: Armando Lindner

Spanish linguistic consultant: Lupe Rodríguez Santizo
English linguistic consultant: Stephanie Lawyer

ISBN: 979-8-9866886-1-9

Printed in the United States of America

Armando Lindner is the author of the bilingual stories collection:
The Excessive Waters of the Río de la Plata and Other Narratives, Seattle, 2020

***

The cover photo is one of the 80,000 Buddha images in the Shittaung Temple complex, in Mrauk U, in Myanmar's Rakhine state (inaccessible location to foreigners at time of writing). Photographed by the author in 2017.

****

Armando Lindner es autor de la colección de historias bilingües:
Las excesivas aguas del Río de la Plata y otras narrativas, Seattle, 2020

***

La foto de la portada es una de las ochenta mil imágenes de Buda en el complejo de templos de Shittaung, en Mrauk U, estado de Rakhine en Myanmar (sitio inaccesible para extranjeros en el año de la publicación de este libro). La foto fue tomada por el autor en 2017.

Dedication

This book is a tribute to my patients, whose unwavering determination to survive I so admired and who taught me the meaning of courage. I was often amazed by their generosity of spirit and by the almost cinematic quality of their clinical histories and adventures that inspired some of these stories.

Dedicatoria

Este libro es un homenaje a mis pacientes, de quienes aprendí el significado del coraje, y admiré su inquebrantable impulso de sobrevivencia. Muchas veces he quedado asombrado con su humanidad y con los acontecimientos casi cinematográficos de tantas historias clínicas y aventuras que inspiraron algunos de estos relatos.

Table of Contents / Índice

I – ENGLISH

A BURMESE JOURNEY

Anh Win, a young, slender man with a pensive smile, sat on a bench at the Yangon airport, waiting for our plane, which was late. As he later told us, all around were well-armed soldiers patrolling the large, old-fashioned hall, but he gave them no reason to question him. Like most people there, he wore a white cotton shirt with a light blue traditional longyi and flip-flops. Instead of reviewing the touring plan for his as yet unmet clients, he had been deep in thought, pondering his recent release from his hometown jail.

Our small contingent of four friends from the US and Canada was exhilarated by the imminent landing in the mysterious Asian country we had only imagined in our dreams. Long before our trip, we had faced a dilemma: Was it ethical to visit a nation under military dictatorship, where most major hotels and businesses were owned and controlled by the ruling army? Old Asia hands among our friends were adamant that the working people in the country would welcome, and depend on, foreign visitors. This view eventually prevailed, and we were finally reaching our long-imagined destination.

Our previous attempt to reach Burma had failed years before because of the Christmas Day earthquake and tsunami that saw gigantic waves smashing over Indonesia, Thailand, and Burma and killing over 200,000 people in just minutes. Bangkok-based Burma News, the voice of the anti-military junta exiles, subsequently reported online that thousands of poisonous scorpions had been the first to sense the earthquake when they surfaced on the Yangon University campus. We needed no other reason to cancel our travel plans.

"Welcome to Myanmar," said the eager young man who was waiting with a sign displaying our family names. "I'm Anh Win, your guide. First, let me help with your documents and customs. My driver is in a van outside, waiting to take you to your hotel." Clearly well prepared and resourceful, Anh Win immediately took charge: within minutes, we were being driven over the tired asphalt of the capital city. Having come from Bangkok, with its neon skyscrapers and Skytrain, arriving in Yangon was like stepping back in time to a colonial city that had seen little change in the last century. We were soon captivated by the hustle and bustle and colorful crowds. Suddenly, as we turned down a long sloping avenue, we had our first glimpse of a colossal golden stupa glistening against the smog of the populous city. I was tempted to jump off the van to go and explore Shwedagon, the country's main Buddhist temple and the high point of our trip.

But I restrained myself, recalling that our friend Marianna had advised us to climb the countless steps at 5-6, in the morning mist, like the most devout of pilgrims.

Our hotel, which was called the Governor's Residence, was another step back in history, this time to the Raj, when the British ruled the Indian subcontinent and Burma until the mid-twentieth century. The building was a romantic, colonial-style mansion dating from the 1920s. We sat in a lush garden dotted with lotus pools, enjoying both a welcome drink and the tropical fragrances carried on the balmy breeze. As I breathed in deeply, I could smell orchids, red torch ginger, and the native *amherstia nobilis*, also known here as the "queen of flowering trees."

Introductions followed. Our guide found our names hard to pronounce, so to break the ice I said, "We like your name, Anh Win. It has a nice rhythm. What does it mean?"

"It means bright and intelligent, both common names in Myanmar."

"Should we say Myanmar or Burma?"

"The Brits used to call it Burma, but today our government prefers Myanmar. If you don't mind, using the modern name may be preferable."

He paused. "Dinner will be served soon by the garden. Later, you may want to take a seat at the Kipling Bar. I will be here at 8 tomorrow morning, after breakfast, to take you to the Shwedagon Pagoda, our most important landmark."

In fiction, the leading character is required

to overcome obstacles. In the 1920s, when Somerset Maugham first visited the city (then known as Rangoon), he almost missed seeing the Shwedagon, "for the Burmese had certain regulations that the Buddhist faith did not demand, and to humiliate the occidentals was the object of the regulations." Indeed, the Burmese thoroughly disliked their British colonizers. My personal challenge, though, was climbing the long staircase in my bare feet, as I suffered from severe plantar fasciitis. Once at the top, I marveled at the sight of a throng of Buddhist visitors spread upon a wide terrace dotted with innumerable shrines and pagodas. The scene had the chaotic feel of a village market. Barefooted men and women drifted silently by, lighting candles or attaching small squares of gold leaf to buddhas of all sizes. Here and there, sitting crossed-legged in the shadows, were saffron-robbed monks deep in meditation. I could not detect any sign that they were breathing as their chests were completely still. This level of meditation was possibly unattainable for us westerners.

No other place in town could match Shwedagon's kaleidoscopic extravagance, its spirituality, and the awe it induces in the visitor. Even so, it was time to move on to new horizons. Once back on the streets, Anh Win sat with us in a tea house nearby to go over the next part of our itinerary: a short flight to Sittwe, on the Andaman Sea, where we would take a river boat to the ancient ruins of

Mrauk U deep in the jungle. His announcement recalled images of Sittwe I had seen online: a dusty tropical enclave with huge bats hanging upside down from tall trees that towered over the town's streets.

I had also seen a video posted by a German traveler that showed a lively barbershop, where dark-skinned hairdressers dried the customers' hair by hand with bamboo paper fans, because most of the country lacked electricity and electrical tools could not be depended on. I was a photographer, and this barbershop was my destination of choice.

Sittwe gave us a glimpse of what Southeast Asia must have been before the two World Wars. The setting of this frontier town reminded me of the black-and-white film, *The Burmese Harp*. I remembered the Japanese soldier who refuses to believe the war is over, and the desolate monks with shaven heads drifting through an infinite landscape, unsure whether they were still alive, or ghosts.

Our expert guide agreed to my request to take an open *tuk-tuk,* large enough for all of us, for exploring the dusty streets. I needed an unobstructed view for my camera and a more immediate connection with the town. We spent a few minutes roaming, our eyes wide, before coming across the barbershop I was searching for. Though small, it was a treasure trove for any photographer obsessed with recording the human element. The barbers were slimmer and darker than Anh Win or other Burmese we had seen so far. They all had a haunted expression, a passivity that suggested depths of suffering. Their gaze reminded me of a dog beaten by its owner and fearful of other humans. They were Rohingya, the descendants of predominantly Muslim Bangladeshi immigrants who arrived several generations back. Referred to as "Bengalis," this minority has never been accepted as true Burmese. They continue to be undocumented, without rights to social services, water, or medical care. I had read in an English newspaper that just a couple of weeks earlier, an unrestrained Buddhist lynch mob had rioted on this main street, possibly even in front of this very barbershop. They had then killed a Rohingya man falsely accused of raping a Burmese woman.

To improve my chances of coming away with the images I was after, I decided to pay one of the barbers five times the cost of a regular service so he would allow me to sit on his chair, pretending to have my hair cut, and take my time photographing the small place. Exhilarated, I clicked away on my Leica, focusing on the barbers and their clients. As I had seen in the video, after washing their customers' hair, the barbers efficiently dried it by hand with a fan. Their elegant movements would spark the envy on any Spanish lady strolling on the Ramblas of Barcelona.

A lonely electric hair dryer lay unused on a counter.

Anh Win interacted with the Rohingya in his usual relaxed and open manner. Later he explained that the prime minister, Aung San Suu Kyi (whom he respectfully called "the Lady,") wished to protect the Rohingya from the military rulers. This was hard to do since she remained under home detention. Anh Win was reluctant to openly criticize the army, but it was obvious he belonged to the silent opposition. Like many Burmese, he revered the Lady and had high hopes for a freer future in Myanmar. Little did we know that the Rohingyas' situation was about to change dramatically and for the worse. Or that the military would stage a violent *coup d'état* a few years later, declare martial law, and indiscriminately kill hundreds of unarmed protesters.

Sittwe was our starting point for getting to Mrauk U, a remote and fabled city that had been re-discovered only a quarter century ago. Back then, taking the dawn ferry for a six-hour journey up the Kaladan River was the only way to travel to Mrauk U. Very few people have ever visited because it is such a challenge to get there, but Anh Win had chartered a river boat that had also seen better days. Its skipper and two sailors, both smiley young Burmese men, kept to themselves as they carefully watched the river traffic. The channel became narrower the farther up-river we went. From time to time, ancient pagodas loomed above the water. Soon, it got dark and then pitch black. It was a starless night so the banks on either side were invisible, except that here and there we saw cooking fires out in the fields. We noticed with alarm that the boat had no on-board lights (except for a weak one in the head) nor even navigation lights. Yet, at times we could feel and hear another barge passing us in the opposite direction, possibly within just a few feet. Either these sailors had extraordinary eyesight or else they had memorized the river bends. At one point, I used my powerful flashlight on the port side but was immediately told to turn it off so as not to disturb the crew's night vision.

It was a very peaceful ride as we were unable to read or move around and were forced into something close to a meditative state. Eventually, there was a little commotion as we arrived at a hotel in the jungle, where porters awaited us to show us to our bungalows.

Accommodations would probably not have been much different in old colonial days, when the British who worked with the East Indian Company got to their isolated jungle stations to supervise logging or mining operations that produced teak or rubies for export. Next morning, a young man advised us to stay clear of the gorgeous pond in front of us because of its poisonous snakes. Soon after breakfast, Anh Win had a van with a driver ready to take us to the dusty local market. We found rows of seamstresses and tailors using pedal-operated sewing machines; an ancient monk buying a bouquet of exotic flowers and nonchalantly pulling out handfuls of local money with which to make his purchase; and food merchants everywhere, selling exotic staples we had never seen before. A man was making a bloody display of killing chickens with a cleaver, before placing their carcasses for sale directly on the muddy soil. I made up my mind right then and there never to eat chicken while in Myanmar.

We were excited to get to Mrauk U in war-torn Rakhine State. Man Pa, the Arakan king, had founded Mrauk U in approximately 1535. By 1780, this independent kingdom extended for more than 400 miles along the coastal plains and mangrove marshlands bordering the Bay of Bengal. In the walled city itself, both Muslims and Buddhists served side by side at the royal court. Dutch, Portuguese, Chinese, and other foreign merchants dwelled in their own prosperous quarter, trading spices, textiles, opium, sulfur, and pepper for rice and ivory. Those glory days ended in 1784, when Burmese invaders crossed the range of hills and conquered Mrauk U. The city and its myriad temples went dark until early 1994, when the cash-strapped military dictatorship sensed the possibilities in tourism and cautiously opened the area to foreigners.

While the better-known ruins of Bagan had been partly restored, Mrauk U itself remained untouched. Temples were interspersed with villages throughout a sleepy rural landscape. In the late afternoon, we climbed a crumbling trail though the forest to the top of a hill. We found ourselves near the still functioning Shitthaung Temple of the 80,000 Buddhas, surrounded by countless pagodas and stupas. When sunset fell, we saw the bluish smoke of cooking fires spreading over the vastness of the valley below. This exquisite network of Buddhist temples and military wall defenses has been proposed as a UNESCO World Heritage site. Tragically, after the Rohingya genocide in 2019, fighting broke out again between the Arakan liberation army and the military regime. The entire province is again off limits to foreign visitors.

On our return downriver to Sittwe, the old ferry in front of us suddenly became a ghost boat as it chugged its way through the dense morning fog. We followed it for a while, watching it turn right around a bend in the river a half mile ahead. A mirage caused by the morning fog made it appear the ferry was magically gliding over the rice paddies—and then it was gone. Later, when the river narrowed again, I was struck by the similarity of our ride to the trip down the Amazon in *Fitzcarraldo,* the Werner Herzog movie. In one unforgettable scene, as the protagonists slowly cruise through the primeval jungle, broadcasting Verdi arias sung by Caruso on an old RCA Victor Gramophone, the Indians on the shore listen, mesmerized and incredulous. On an impulse, I asked Anh Win to loan me his mini speakers so I could play music aloud from my smart phone. As the improbable melodies of an Argentine tango spread through the Burmese forest, my wife and I spontaneously got up to dance, still wearing our muddy boots, on the rotting wooden deck.

As we returned to the Rohingya village port we had left earlier that day, we encountered a nearly medieval scene: a long single file of half-naked men and a few women carrying heavy loads of river rocks over their heads up a steep ramp, from the water to a low hill on the shore. Most of them were barefooted, a few had flip-flops, and they seemed malnourished and destitute. We learned that this poorly paid job produced the small, water-polished rocks widely used for gardens, roads, hearths, or decoration. I made a mental note about the importance of being mindful that rocks of this kind had been stained by the sweat of slaves in all but name from this and other villages.

As we drove back to the hotel, we slowly passed a loud group of protesters near a village on the main road. Many of the men wore skullcaps, a telltale sign that they were Muslim. I was so impressed by this sight that I asked our driver to stop so I could photograph them. But Anh Min, clearly alarmed, immediately ordered him to speed on by. Outside the village proper, we had to show our documents at a military roadblock. As we were the only tourists in the area, they let us pass. But I noticed the sweat on Anh Min's neck and realized it was the first time I had seen him perspire despite the very hot weather throughout the trip.

Once we were safely back at the hotel lounge, I invited our guide to share a cup of tea with us. I wanted to understand his distress at the roadblock. I hoped that by this time he would be able to trust our discretion.

"I'm troubled because I was thrown in jail and then released just before your group arrived. While waiting at the airport, with soldiers everywhere, I was thinking about this and couldn't concentrate on the details of your tour. It was painful for me and for my family, especially for my mom."

"Why did they pick you up, Anh Win? Was it political?"

"No, a corrupt policeman in my hometown stopped me on the road when I was giving a tourist a ride on my motorcycle. He was a client I knew well who had wanted to explore more of the ruins there and had called me from the airport asking me to take him. I could not refuse."

"Why would they put you in jail? You are an accredited guide who's well known in your village."

"There's a security rule prohibiting driving with a foreigner on the back of a motorcycle. Nobody pays attention to it, but the policeman insisted on fining me, and I refused to pay. The tourist could not help and had to walk the rest of the way with his backpack. I managed to give him my mom's number so he could phone her and let her know."

"How long did they keep you? How did you get out?"

"I was in jail for a week. The first day was terrible because the only thing they gave me to eat was some stale rice, and the water was dirty. I was afraid of getting sick. Some of the other prisoners weren't feeling well and there was no medical care."

"How was your mother able to help?"

"Our family has been here for many generations and we have a large furniture factory. We use teak and other exotic woods and export the furniture to China. But, in the old days, our grandfather was involved in mining for precious stones, and we had some rubies of different sizes hidden away. Mom picked two of the nicest stones and went to the police chief in our town, who she knew. He was abusive, but she was able to pacify him with a bribe. Later, they let her bring me some homemade food and a case of bottled water. I was not beaten, but the police and other prisoners harassed me all the time, until they moved me to a smaller cell by myself, and I felt safer then. Finally, they let me go, but I'm still anxious when I'm near the police. They know we sympathize with the opposition, that our family supports 'the Lady.' We must be careful, so please keep this to yourselves."

Anh Win seemed pleased to have a shoulder to lean on, and he began to trust and appreciate our company. He invited us to visit their factory and meet his family. His mother was an elegant woman in early middle age, who had great poise and determination. Clearly, she would have the skills necessary for neutralizing a corrupt chief of police. As we toured the workshop, we realized the quality and the craftmanship were astonishing: everything was hand- made. The foreman, who spoke good English, explained that electricity was intermittent and replacement parts for most tools are hard to find. They did not trust power tools, but they could always depend on their own hands. They were proud of their work and afraid that relying upon electrical equipment would lead them to lose the skills passed on by previous generations. We observed the same reasoning, and superlative craftmanship, all over the country among artisans, carpenters, boat builders, cigar makers, and in particular jewelers, who were capable of doing exquisite filigree work with precious metals.

Our interest (mine in particular) in Buddhist ritual and philosophy, as well as meditation practices, must have made an impression on Anh Win. One morning, after fumbling with his phone for a few minutes, he came up with a surprising suggestion: "My Buddhist master, the abbot of the Mahāganhāyon monastery in Mandalay, just answered that he is willing to see us for a private meeting. He speaks good English. Should I include this in our itinerary for tomorrow?"

We were delighted by this unique opportunity. The monastery was amid a tropical, green paradise in Amarapura. We arrived before 11 AM, which was lunch hour for both the student monks and nuns (who resided across the street) and watched them line up, quiet and orderly, for their only meal of the day.

After their lunch, we took a relaxing walk through the monastery, at times accompanied by lively groups of novices. Anh Win had instructed us to address his mentor as "Hashin" (which sounded curiously to us like "Ha Shem," literally "The Name" in Judaism, a reference to God).

Hashin was a smiley, slim, youthful man of about 40, just back from a six-month meditation retreat in the jungle in Shan State.

After a cursory introduction, his deep gaze and attentiveness suggested he had already assessed our interest and was ready to begin the session. We sat on a hard concrete floor, mostly with legs crossed in observance of the rule never to point our feet at the master, which would be a sign of disrespect. Given my age, stiff joints, and painful arthritis, I quickly realized I was no longer made for a prolonged stay at the monastery. But I did my best to ignore my discomfort and to pay attention. Although Hashin was eager to answer questions, soon his speech evolved into a monologue:

"I have taught *Vipasāna,* or mindfulness meditation, to many foreign students who stayed with us for ten days, but in just one hour I can only give you basic instructions. This practice makes our minds pure, and calm. Buddhists in old age must find self-understanding and self-reliance when they approach death.

"You must learn how to sit and use breathing meditation for at least a half hour to start observing your sensations. You are not allowed to control your breathing or your mind. You should observe them as they are and not try to change them deliberately. After a half hour, we generally continue with a walking meditation, and both sitting and standing practices should be done mindfully and in silence. You must observe but not modify any distracting thoughts to eventually realize the impermanent nature of mind and matter, till you achieve the contemplation of Dhamma. To me, meditation means to observe oneself deeply to attain true wisdom."

After this short but intense encounter, we purchased several books by Hashin about Buddhism and democracy, current events, and even the philosophy of married life. Had I known that, a few weeks after our visit, Buddhist monks and the military would begin to exterminate a large part of the Rohingya population, I would have asked for his opinion on these matters. The village of Buthidaung, and the temple we had visited and photographed, had been strafed by a Burmese gunship in 2019. What would he have to say about "the Lady," who would receive a Nobel Prize for her opposition to the junta? Incomprehensibly, she later denied the facts of the persecution before the United Nations and instead sided with the military. Despite her support of the armed forces, Aung San Suu Kyi was arrested in 2021 during the coup and, as I write, her whereabouts are unknown.

Getting to our destination at Inle lake was an example of Anh Win's tenacious character and resourcefulness. Because the roads are muddy and have huge potholes, it's best to arrive at the hotel by boat from Nyaungshwe, the gateway village to the lake. These long boats, with a row of three to four single seats that runs lengthwise down the middle, are usually owned by the military, who have a monopoly on most private property. In recent years, a few daring civilians had set up smaller tour companies that compete with the cartels. Thus, Anh Win had himself invested in a new boat; with the initial profits, he had been able to expand and now owned eight small vessels on the lake. He had the courage to lock horns with the authorities and was able to take us to the hotel in a brand-new craft from his small fleet. We arrived safely, although we had secretly feared an attack by a military boarding party with grappling hooks.

One morning Anh Win took us to the Hpaung Daw U Pagoda, on a tiny island, about a city block in diameter, in the middle of the lake. The small port was literally mobbed by many similar long boats bringing the relatives of young monks who were about to be ordained in the historic Buddhist temple. We were soon surrounded by throngs of family members of all ages, but even so we managed to watch the bright, colorful ceremony from the main inside gate. In this unique setting, we found the devotion of the families, and the significance of the moment, to be quite moving. Unfortunately, the situation took an unexpectedly urgent turn, when needing to relieve myself, I went in search of the toilets. In the main hallway, the two separate bathrooms for men and woman each had a long line of people waiting, all clearly with the same intention. I looked around outside, but there wasn't a single tree to hide behind, and a crowd of villagers were wandering about on the trail. I had no option but to line up for my turn at the sacred pissing grounds, still barefooted as required at the temple. To my dismay, the drains in both toilets were plugged up, and the small room was overflowing with pungent, dark, yellow urine rising several inches above ground. Given the size of my prostate, and the urgency of the situation, I had to bite the bullet and dive in with the other villagers, who found the flood disconcerting but less surprising. It took me a long time and a whole bar of soap under the hotel shower to clean off the redolent

Burmese urine.

The two weeks in Burma were transformative and opened my eyes and heart to the humanity of the Burmese people, their spirituality, grace, and talent. We owed much to our well-trained, ingenious gentleman of a guide and enterprising boater of Inle lake. A lot of water has flowed under the bridge in the last few years as the country has witnessed profound changes. I'm grateful to the Rohingya communities in the villages, and to the barbers who so kindly allowed me to record a moment of their daily life with my photographs. But I am acutely anxious about their survival since this ethnic group has suffered extermination and expulsion to Bangladesh and the largest refugee camp in the world. In the recent weeks, BBC News has shown distressing images of a bloody repression by the army on the streets of Yangon, Mandalay, and other cities. All of this during a murderous pandemic for which there cannot be relief under this unprepared regime. I hope that these catastrophic events may soon come to an end and that the leaders responsible will be brought to justice. My wife and I dream we may, once again, climb barefooted and without pain up the innumerable steps to the Shwedagon.

MILANESAS

As I was walking through a neighborhood I normally did not go to, near the Chancellery in Plaza San Martín, the pangs in my belly reminded me that it was past noon and time to look for a place to have lunch. As is often the case in Buenos Aires, there was a café on the corner where the menu of the day had been written out by hand and posted in the window. I went in without looking it over because the neat and clean appearance of the place appealed to me and because there were tables still available. I was on a lightning trip to visit my mother, who was in hospital with heart failure. This time she was in no position to prepare one of her unforgettable dishes for me.

I took a seat by a window and soon after the waiter showed up to take my order.

"What can I offer you, sir?" he asked me kindly.

"What do you suggest? I'm not from the neighborhood so I don't know what your specialties are."

"Well, there are only two choices, and today I recommend the milanesas with French fries. The young man in the kitchen makes them as if that's what he'd been born to do! Would you like them plain or a caballo?"

"Plain, please, and with lots of lemon." His question made me smile, because adding a fried egg on top of the meat, and calling it a caballo (on horseback), was a typical Argentine expression.

While I was waiting for my food to arrive, I watched the passersby and thought about the memorable taste of milanesas—and the day long ago when I was still doing my medical residency and had turned up at my grandmother's house for lunch to eat this very same dish. An almost surreal situation had unfolded, and I was free because the hospital was closed due to a strike by non-medical personnel at the university. I also thought about the skill of Argentine waiters, who rarely need to write down orders, even complicated ones for a large table, and yet never forget what each person has asked for. Argentine customs, learned in my childhood, were very different from those I had become accustomed to after so many years in the United States. Reacquainting myself with these practices made me feel at home again, since I had been born and raised here—although at times I had a strange feeling of *depaysement*, the novelty and disorientation brought on by a change of scene.

And then the order arrived, a succulent golden milanesa, accompanied by glistening crispy fries and surrounded by slices of very yellow lemon. The colorful palette stirred my unchecked imagination to transform the dish into a rustic painting as textured as a Matisse or a Van Gogh painting. I relished the delicacy for a long time, until the waiter came back to offer me the usual *cafecito* to complete the meal.

After the generous feast, I strolled aimlessly around the city, remembering old walks and happy, or sometimes painful, coincidences, in which other milanesas made an unexpected appearance. One such event had happened on another trip to visit my mother, whose stays in the hospital, and more recently in intensive care, had become increasingly frequent. On one of these occasions, my wife and I took advantage of some free time in Buenos Aires to ask Rubén, our dear tango teacher, to give us a private lesson. We agreed to meet him at the corner of Entre Ríos and San Juan, a popular neighborhood very close to my old high school that I had known well when I was young. Everything there now seemed as dilapidated as in a wartime movie, both the buildings and some of the residents. We arrived early to walk around the neighborhood and marveled at a large colored mural on a street corner. It showed an antique projector, the emblem of the Cafe del Biógrafo, the term originally used for movie theaters. As though caught in a planetary magnetic field, I was drawn to the handwritten sign in the window: "Dish of the day: Milanesas, Napolitan-style." Once inside, we saw women with children running between the tables, and a local customer, who was well advanced in years, sound asleep over a newspaper provided by the establishment. On his table was an empty espresso cup, probably the minimum purchase required for him to linger there for hours. The price of food seemed very reasonable to us tourists, so we asked for two orders of milanesas, which turned out to be a huge portion. The cutlets had overlapping layers of mozzarella, cooked ham, and a tasty tomato sauce that the locals call "tuco." The size of this feast might have fed an entire family of starving refugees just off the freighter in the nearby port. It would have been foolish to waste any of it, and we thought of taking the leftovers back to the hotel for dinner. This custom, so common in the United States, immediately provoked an unheard-of quarrel with the waiter.

"Do you really want to take the leftovers? People don't do that here. Sometimes the guys in the kitchen want to finish them or we throw them away. Besides, I don't have any containers to put them in. Nobody asks for them."

"No offense meant! The milanesas were great, but we had a very late breakfast and now we're too full to finish them. It would be a crime not to take them home. Look, we don't mind if you put them in the cartons you use for pizza. I see you have a lot of those." He reluctantly agreed to this and of course we left a substantial tip. Then we walked to our lesson, feeling very proud of the culinary prize in the box we were carrying.

We found Ruben on the main corner of the barrio and headed to the apartment belonging to Melinda, his colleague and partner for this lesson. She lived in a nicely painted multi-story house, but with a curious entrance enclosed by a large wrought-iron cage that had two consecutive locked doors, like a police cell in a small town in Wyoming. Around the enclosure some characters were lying on the floor sound asleep, or maybe they were junkies who had overdosed, which may have explained the measures the neighbors had taken to protect themselves. We entered an apartment that was almost empty except for the mirrors for the dancers, placed the cardboard box on a table, and never thought about it again. The scene at the entrance had been very unpleasant, but we managed to forget it during Ruben's wonderful tango lesson.

As I practiced some new steps and corrected my mistakes, I was distracted by the atmosphere of the place, which brought back memories of my adolescence in a similar apartment in the barrio of Barracas. Then as now, we could hear, through open windows facing an inner courtyard, the snatches of conversation between neighbors, and take in the intense aroma of good food drifting up from the lower floors. We imagined it being prepared by an excellent neighborhood cook. When class was almost over, we suddenly noticed that the sky had become leaden and the light was decreasing rapidly. Without warning, a terrifying tempest—lightning, thunder and torrential rain—unleashed itself as happens sometimes in the capital or in the province of Buenos Aires. We looked out on the street, which was already flooded and almost completely empty of vehicles. Ruben and his partner were alarmed for us and proposed that we finish the lesson at once. We hurriedly paid them and rushed towards the exit, where Ruben opened the double locks of the cage for us to get out. The junkies were still asleep and oblivious to the flood. Miraculously, a taxi stopped in front of the entrance and, as soon as the passenger got out, we scrambled into the back seat without waiting to check if it was alright with the driver. The taxi headed towards the hotel, almost floating down Avenida Entre Ríos. We congratulated ourselves on our good luck, and then, as we passed Congress, we suddenly and very sadly discovered that we had forgotten the cardboard box with what was left of our lunch, and knew that it would be impossible to retrieve it in the middle of the tropical downpour. At the same time, we realized that the delicious aroma that had distracted us during our lesson had come from our box with its "Milanesas, Napolitan-style" label. Sadder still, Ruben called the following morning to thank me for the wonderful lunch we had left for them, which they discovered after class.

The next day, after visiting my mother at the hospital, I impulsively decided to phone the few friends I still had left in Buenos Aires, including Victoria, a pal from my university days. She had been born in Patagonia and grown up on her family's farm near El Bolsón in Río Negro. After studying at the University of Buenos Aires, like many young people she had decided to live in the capital and only went back to Patagonia in the summer and for holidays with her family. Her brothers took care of the raising and management of thousands of sheep scattered throughout their extensive property.

Victoria had published several books of poetry, won prizes from the Catholic University, and been published in the renowned Journal of Poetry. We shared memories from our student days when we backpacked in the south of the country, a mutual appreciation for Patagonia, and especially our love of literature (although I was interested in prose and fiction while she preferred poetry). Victoria welcomed me that same afternoon with a glass of wine so we could bring each other up to date about our life experiences and other important events.

"As you know, Alberto and I divorced two years ago. Like others of our generation, he went back to the countryside to raise sheep. But frankly, I love urban life and the intellectual opportunities of this great city," she explained. Of course, I thought, she had the luxury of being able to write poetry fulltime thanks to her financial independence and her brothers' willingness to manage the estate in the south.

"I'm surprised you don't want to spend more time in El Bolsón. I remember it as a beautiful place with many natural and cultural attractions, and the town has a reputation for being interesting and progressive."

"It's true that tourists like it a lot, with its market of regional crafts, wool and leather goods, and creole knives among other things. But for us, what's most important is to have declared ourselves a "nuclear-free zone" and completely limit any radioactive pollution. In this, we're unique in the country. On the other hand, we're concerned about a possible eruption of the Chaitén, the volcano on the Chilean side of the Andes. Due to the mountain winds, volcanic ash frequently rains down onto nearby villages, which sometimes have to be evacuated. As you know, Chile has the largest and most active chain of volcanoes in the world after Indonesia. I'm extremely worried for my people in Patagonia."

"I suppose you must have a new partner by now?" I asked, not very tactfully, to change the subject. I didn't think the volcano was that serious, though her anxiety was understandable. Like other poets, Victoria was quite sensitive and tended to be overdramatic.

"Actually, I don't have a steady partner. I sometimes go out with Facundo, a professional polo player who travels a lot around the world to compete. He's the team captain and a very popular guy, who doesn't have the slightest intention of being trapped by a divorcee. Look, I don't mean to interrupt our chat, but tonight there's a meeting of the Buenos Aires Poetry Society, an organization I like. They meet at a bookstore in Palermo. Would you like to join me? There may be some interesting readings and you might meet some engaging people. We just wouldn't have time for dinner before the meeting. What do you think?" "I love the idea if I don't have to participate in the discussion. I know as much about poetry as I do about quantum physics."

The bookstore was well-stocked in Spanish language literature, especially from Latin America, and I thought I'd come back another day and choose some books to take home with me. About a hundred people of different ages, some of whom were couples, sat around in chairs arranged in a messy semicircle.

Many of the younger ones wore intense, intelligent expressions, dressed unpretentiously, and favored long hair. Others, not so young and somewhat more professorial, sat toward the front near the center of the room, where there was a small table with good light to read by and present their work. One very serious man with disheveled grey hair sat somewhat apart from the rest, as if the others had made room for him out of respect. Or maybe they were reluctant to approach him.

The program included several readings followed by a few minutes of questions or brief comments for the poet. I did not know any of the writers and it was hard for me to catch their names. The questions were generally about technique, and polite, as though everyone there were a part of a family—but sometimes they were sharper and more aggressive. There were no cell phones to record presentations in those days, so I was forced to write quickly with a pencil or use shorthand.

A chubby middle-aged man with the peaceful demeanor of a Buddhist monk, who was introduced as "Padeletti," read his poem, "Inscriptions in the Ashram," which struck me as exotic and profound. Here is a loose English translation of a short but touching fragment I managed to write down:

> If everything is different,
> then all is nothing and all is everything:
> in the grain the pomegranate,

a ruby, beehive, blood and saber stroke.
The stone the alchemist was searching for,
 is, under any name, before the eyes,
 not the secret, only its form…

A little later a young woman who, like Victoria, had been raised in Patagonia, took the stage. A short brunette with large eyes as black as coal, she energetically recited her poem, "Protections." Again, I was able to write down a few lines:

Protection, and all the books I loved
A crucifix to scare away skeletons
A trail of yellow leaves
For a bike ride in the fall.

And then she offered the audience a few Impressions of a pleasant childhood in a country cottage:

Aged alcoholic spirits
Plum marmalade in the kitchen
And a little place by the fireplace
To pull the strings of silence
At the time of the apparition stories

When the reading was over, it was close to midnight and most people had left. The few who had stayed behind were scattered around the bookstore. Victoria joined a smaller group and invited me to continue the discussion at a neighborhood café. I accepted, grateful to be included. A little later, when my friend introduced me at the café, the group welcomed me with curiosity and with a kiss, a greeting that is second nature in Argentina and not just among poets. Before I left the country as a young man, this custom, so different from the Anglo-Saxon conventions, was rare among men. But now, it helped to immediately put me at ease.

Soon the waiter came to take our orders, which were very straightforward: coffee for everyone. Except that I hadn't eaten since lunchtime and so I thoughtlessly ordered one of my favorite dishes: a milanesa sandwich, something very common in Buenos Aires cafes. The unexpected request produced a commotion at the table, and several people glared at me in disapproval. But I made a quick recovery: "I apologize. I'm Victoria's guest. I've been overseas for so many years, I'm not familiar with what happens after readings like this one. Would you allow me to treat you all to something to eat?"

At first the group's response was tentative. Then they slowly began to raise their hands, reminding me of the swell of an ocean wave, and a few seconds later the whole table agreed to ask for ¡The same for everyone! It was obvious that the economic situation in Argentina at the time meant that young poets and the mentors they admired could not afford more than a simple coffee.

Although I wanted to get to know more about their interests and personalities, I had to respond to their surprise, curiosity, and gratitude for the unexpected offer. Several of them assumed that I was also a poet, but I explained, defending myself as well as I could, that I wrote short stories and was not skilled in writing poetry. The respectable gray-haired gentleman slouched on the chair in front of me was almost asleep and not part of the conversation. The woman who had read the poem about her youth in Patagonia was one of the first to question me:

"Have you ever traveled through Patagonia? You may have recognized certain places in my poem."

"Yes, I remember going through El Bolson when I was backpacking as a student. I would have liked to go back and stay longer. Your poem really impressed me with its homey childhood images, such as the references to 'plum candy in the kitchen; a little place near the fireplace…at the time of the apparition's stories'. The latter is a strong description of a scene that I can imagine but have never experienced. Who in your house told these kinds of stories to frighten children?"

"I'm amazed that you remember something I recited so quickly! My father used to invite the foreman of the ranch to join us because he was a *payador* who improvised as he recited, played the guitar, and was a good storyteller. We could make him talk all night by giving him a shot of sugarcane brandy."

The conversation seemed to revive the gray-haired gentleman, who woke up and then, out of the blue, asked me, "Are you going to tell us what your favorite themes are for your short stories?"

Before I could answer, Victoria beat me to it: "I have something to say about Armando's story, *The*

Parallel Death of Don Quixote, because he doesn't know the details about what happened. It's about a dramatic meeting of two forensic doctors and old friends who are at a restaurant on Lake Washington. He wrote it in English and asked me to translate it into Spanish. When I worked on it, I liked its imaginative, surreal elements. Without asking for his permission, I took the liberty of sending it to a literary competition being held by the Argentine Society of Science Fiction. As you may have guessed by now, it won the first place! Because Armando was in the United States, his mother, who had never read the story, had to accept the award on his behalf. Since she didn't know what it was about, she felt honored to do so but was unable to say anything about the story. Worse yet, that was the society's last get-together, because it was dissolved at the end of the year: 'Sic transit gloria mundi!'"

The serious professorial gentleman gradually became more alert and began taking part in the conversation. He looked at me and said, "You should write about the people at this meeting today. We might give you some dramatic material for a short story. And ... as a corollary to your earlier invitation, can you explain the meaning of the expression "the truth of the milanesa," if you know it?

"Thank you for reminding me of this popular idiom. I didn't know it was still in use since language evolves. I take it to be a metaphor for life in general. But I don't want to disappoint you with an insufficient response. Instead, I prefer to quote what Padeletti said today: "Everything is nothing and all is everything" when he suggested that "The stone the alchemist was looking for is, under any name, before the eyes." You've inspired me to write about this trip and about tonight. I hope to find an adequate answer to your question one day."

Stimulated by the coffee and the milanesas, which had not only broken the ice but energized the group, the talk continued for a while. In my case, it helped establish a rapport with some of them and made me feel comfortable in this environment. Being part of this group allowed me to relive the experiences of my youth in Buenos Aires which—like my years spent living abroad—had contributed to my emotional development.

Inevitably, the evening came to an end and people started to get up from their seats. The grey-haired man, whose name I did not yet know, came over to say goodbye and, to my great surprise, gave me a big hug and a kiss on the left cheek, before saying simply: "Good luck with everything, and keep on writing!" Then he took off without acknowledging anyone else. Most of the poets in the room were speechless, and Victoria hurried to tell me in disbelief: "Do you realize you're the only one who Diego, the dean of Argentine poetry, kissed goodbye, something he almost never does—and you're the only person he didn't know at this meeting! It's incredible and maybe meant as an insult to the rest of us. He seemed quite depressed, although that's nothing new. For some reason you made a strong impression in him."

When we said goodbye outside her house, I thanked Victoria for introducing me to these fascinating, clever people. Then, already feeling wistful about this very special moment, and even a little sad about leaving my friend, I made my way to my hotel nearby. I had only two days left before my return home, and I was hopeful that my mother would improve and be discharged from the hospital.

While waiting for a taxi at the hotel entrance on the day of my departure, the young man from the reception rushed over to me to let me know I had a phone call. It was Victoria, who was beside herself. Her voice broke as she delivered her message.

"Armando, I'm sorry to be the bearer of bad news before you leave! I just learned that the morning after the poetry meeting Diego's secretary found him dead at his desk. He shot himself! This is a great tragedy for Argentine poetry. He had no other family, and we were probably the last people to talk to him before he committed suicide. As if this weren't bad enough, I also must leave Buenos Aires, because the Chaitén has become increasingly active and my people need me. It's one drama after another."

A few days after my arrival back in Seattle, I read in the New York Times that all flights over Patagonia had been cancelled because the Chaitén had erupted in Chile. Volcanic ash, scattered by the southern winds, had particularly affected the Bolson region of Argentina. The large ranches there were covered by a toxic layer of ash that was having severe respiratory and digestive effects on the animals and had already killed thousands of sheep that could not find clean water and vegetation. I feared that the news would have a terrible long-term effect on Victoria and on her property. After that we lost touch, and I never received any response to my messages. I sense that this tragedy is connected in an unfathomable way to Diego's death, to whom I will never be able to explain, even if I could, "the truth of the milanesa."

TARAGÜI ÑE'É

The day the first Allied soldiers landed in Sicily in 1943, Gigí Musumeci fell ill with a second bout of malaria and was unable to celebrate the liberation. He would not be the first: more than ten thousand American soldiers endured a similar fate in the swamps of Catania, which were notorious as the breeding ground for the anopheles mosquito. The casualties from disease exceeded the number of war-wounded and did not include the deaths from dengue and Malta fevers. In those days it was difficult to tell the diseases apart, and the soldiers knew them simply as FUO or fevers of unknown origin. Soon after, tired of war, malaria, and, most of all, hunger and misery, Gigí escaped as a crew member on a cargo ship bound for South America. His first port of call was Buenos Aires. Looking for a way to make a living, and misinformed about Argentina's geography, he continued up the Paraná River in a supply boat that served riverside settlers. Eventually he found work as a fisherman in the impoverished province of Corrientes.

Gigí was confident that he could manage well enough in Spanish because he was familiar with words of Spanish origin used in the Sicilian dialect.

On the other hand, the contacts he made in a community of simple and hard-working but less educated people, many of indigenous origin, spoke mostly an incomprehensible language they called *Taragüí ñe'é*. He later learned that *Taragüí* was the Guaraní name for Corrientes, and that it also meant "lizard," a very fast but shy creature that scuttled all over the white walls. His new friends explained that the Indians spoke mostly *Avañé'é*, or "the human language," to differentiate it from the *Karaiñé'é*, or "word of the lords," as the language of the hated conquerors was known.

In this environment, he learned to communicate mainly in Guaraní and so, like many of his neighbors, never really learned to speak Spanish. He was told that the few soldiers who had arrived from Paraguay and founded Corrientes in 1588 tried to convert the natives and ban the use of the local language. But being outnumbered by the indigenous population forced the Spaniards to learn the Guaraní language instead.

Even so, the locals borrowed Spanish words to refer to numbers, colors, and kinship.

Thanks to his background as a fisherman, Gigi Musumeci was able to survive for years working on the tumultuous Paraná and Paraguay Rivers, which Sebastián Gaboto, the Venetian navigator, had discovered in 1527. The river fish, which could be enormous, were species of unmatched strength and fighting spirit such as the golden dorado, *surubíes,* and *bogas.* But he would never forget fishing in the Mediterranean off

Sicily, between the islands of Favignana and Levanzo, on the glorious day of La Tonnara on April 23, when the sea turned red with the blood of the tuna they killed with sticks. The tuna "slaughters" had enriched only the many Sicilian nobles, but the memory now comforted Gigí in his exile in Corrientes.

He quickly adapted to his new environment because the strong piety of the people and veneration of the saints reminded him of home. The roots of the local conservative culture had a magical component. He would find on the many urban and rural roads, altars decorated with flags and red ribbons next to the picture of a very young gaucho, possibly the victim of a violent and wrongful death. It was explained that this was "Gauchito Gil", a popular saint believed to have produced miracles, and the object of widespread devotion in that area. Taking on this belief as his own, Gigí built a small altar, decorated with red ribbons, on his ranch. On January 8, the saint's feast day, he visited the saint's main shrine in the city of Mercedes along with the hundreds of thousands of pilgrims delivering offerings. Possibly as the result of his prayers, he would soon meet the woman who became his companion.

Fishing along the Parana to the north of the provincial capital, he found himself in the coastal town of Itatí. It was July 16, the feast day of the town's Virgin. Despite the crowds, one evening he found a place in the basilica to sit down to pray, next to a young indigenous girl, who smiled at him. When she spoke, she greeted him in Guaraní with a phrase that was only used after sunset:

"*Mbá eichapá nde pyharé?*" (How are you to-night?)

By then he was familiar with the traditional answer:

"*Che pyharé porâ, ha ndé?*" (Very well. How about you?)

"*Che pyharé porâ avei.*" (Likewise, thank you.)

Her name was Itatí, like the Virgin of the basilica. They continued their conversation in Spanish mixed with several words in Guaraní. Gigí told her about his self-exile from Sicily and his work as a fisherman. He listened with interest to the details of her life in a nearby village. As it happened, her relatives were also fishermen. After a while, Itatí unexpectedly invited him to a village dance:

"*Ejerókisé chendivé?*" (Would you like to dance?)

Surprised, Gigí agreed to accompany her to the party in a nearby cantina, where musicians strolled with an accordion and guitars, happily playing a *chamamé*, a very rhythmic, flowing folk tune that suggested the rolling of the Paraná River. They also improvised with other colonial tunes of European origin, such as the Corrientes polka and the waltz. The accordion reminded him of the traditional music of his people in Sicily and increased his fondness for the locals and their customs.

Itatí turned out to be a good dancer, both spontaneous and natural. Her personality captivated Gigí, who returned to the town several times and eventually bought a little ranch by the river where they settled down together. It was close to his chosen fishing grounds, the main drawback being the hordes of mosquitoes that descended on them every evening as was typical in the tropics. Itatí mixed some ointments to protect herself a little from the bites as well as to soften the itch. But the presence of these insects gave Gigí nightmares that called up memories of his faraway homeland and the swamps of Catania that he would have preferred to leave behind.

Itatí was a very good cook and mastered the local dishes, especially those consisting of fresh dorado or *surubíes* that Gigí brought home after a good day's fishing. On warm evenings, she would wait for him with an iced *tereré* or with a well-prepared mate in a gourd as huge as a melon—a tradition in neighboring Paraguay on the other side of the river. She often served them with fried cakes, or *chipacueritos*, as they were called in Corrientes, made from flour and cow fat. On feast days she would prepare *mbeyú*, which in Guaraní means "flattened cake." It was a native delicacy that used manioc starch, which dated back to the kitchens of the Franciscan Reductions and the Jesuit missions.

Gigí loved fishing in the Paraná and his epic battles with the huge dorados, which were great fighters. Because of his skill, the indigenous people of the area honored him with the nickname Parí, which meant he was expert at catching fish using Guaraní methods while respecting the environment. But he also spent a lot of time in the swampy and unhealthy region of the Iberá marshlands, where he came across fauna of all kinds: mammals, reptiles, batrachians, fish and, worst of all, insects. Sometimes he caught eels, which connoisseurs considered so tasty, and he enjoyed finding the *tamboatás*, small fish about six centimeters long and great devourers of mosquitoes. He never got used to living around the local snakes, the dreaded *yarará* or viper of the cross, or the multi-colored coral snake, which sometimes killed locals and fishermen. But he was delighted to be surrounded by so many birds, the big toucan, the ostriches, the flamingos and *teros*, the woodpeckers and the colorful parrots. This lessened his anxiety and the nightmares brought on by the insects, snakes, and caimans.

A year after they met, Itatí gave birth to a beautiful little girl they called Yrasema, which meant "Rumor of the River," although her friends nicknamed her Inés, which was easier to pronounce. She grew up in the village mostly in the company of her mother's family. Curiously, once she reached adolescence, her Sicilian genes brought out her European features and her light brown hair contrasted with her deep dark eyes. She loved mimicking Gigí's gestures, because he talked with his hands, and sometimes she went fishing with him. Like her mother, she preferred to speak in Guaraní, although she understood quite a lot of Spanish and managed without difficulty at school, learning to read and write with ease. Her parents sent her to high school in the more populous and developed city of Corrientes, where she could stay with her aunts and help them around the house after school. They took her in because Gigí gave them a monthly stipend although his earnings were limited and barely enough to support him and his wife.

At high school Inés had the chance to meet different people and make new friends among the refugees who arrived during and after World War II. When a German student fell ill and stopped attending classes, there were rumors that she was being treated in a remote and secret location by a German "doctor" who was under the protection of President Stroessner in neighboring Paraguay. She never imagined that years later it would be confirmed that the doctor in question was the notorious Dr. Mengele, the Auschwitz criminal.

Ironically, Inés also met Germans of Jewish origin, the children and grandchildren of the survivors of war. It was the first time she had heard the word "Jew" and she understood that some people practiced religions other than Catholicism. She asked a very studious student, Ruth Goldman, if they could study for exams together at her house. Sometimes, she would be invited to stay for lunch afterwards. The bond between the girls grew stronger during their evening strolls together, known as the *vuelta del perro* around the main square. Inés's world gradually expanded, and she discovered that there were also Protestant and other religious minorities in the city. The Jewish community congregated in a downtown synagogue and at the cultural association called Scholem Aleijem. They also had a place for picnics by the river, where Ruth invited her one Sunday to meet other members of the family.

One day Ruth casually mentioned that they wouldn't be able to walk together for a few days because her family was celebrating Pesach, the Jewish Passover, which that year fell a few days before the Christian holiday. She was going to help her mother prepare a traditional dish, a stuffed fish called gefilte fish, made with white fish—preferably carp as in Europe—and whitebait. When Inés heard this, a lightbulb went off in her head as she thought of a way to reciprocate the kindness of the new friends who had made her feel so accepted. She asked Gigí to send her some fresh fish so she could give it to them the following day when her uncle would be delivering the fish to the central market. Her plan worked, and Inés was able to proudly give the fish to Ruth. The gefilte fish was excellent, and Ruth's family said it was the best fish they'd had since their arrival in the country.

The period of calm and happiness, when Inés was almost out of high school, was brief. At that time, she saw very little of her father, who was working hard in the swampy, mosquito-infested area of Iberá. What Gigí always feared in his nightmares, an unexpected second bout of malaria, attacked him with a vengeance. Possibly this time it was caused by the Plasmodium falciparum, a different and more lethal species than the P. Vivax that had infected him as a young man in Sicily. Within hours he became worse and developed cerebral symptoms, and then he went into a deep coma. He was transferred to the central hospital in Corrientes, where they had only quinine for treating his fever. So, some fifteen years after his arrival in Corrientes, Gigí succumbed to a final attack of malaria, which was endemic in the province that had sheltered him during the war.

This tragedy drastically transformed the lives of Inés and Itatí, who was left with no resources for supporting her daughter. Without Gigí's contributions, Inés's aunts no longer had any incentive to take her in. She soon dropped out of school and was reduced to looking for work as a servant, because job opportunities for a young indigenous girl in the upper Paraná were virtually nonexistent.

As the weeks went by, Inés, despite her optimistic and cheerful character, gradually fell into a depression. Then, one sunny Saturday morning, when she was off work, her friend Ruth showed up unexpectedly.

"*Maitei, Inés dear, mba eichapá?*"

"*Maitei*, Ruth, it's terrible. I'm in such financial difficulty and sad that I can't keep studying. "

"I'm so sorry, but I have an idea that could help."

"I don't think so, Ruth. There's nothing to be done," Inés answered in despair.

"Of course there is! Look, come to the picnic at the cultural association tomorrow. I really want you to meet some friends who are here from Buenos Aires. It's important that you come well dressed. I'll pick you up in Dad's car, that powerful Ford 39 that he lets me drive—as you know, that's unusual for a girl in the provinces. Let's make an entrance like two queens! We have to impress the visitors too."

At the picnic, Inés noticed she was being stared at more than usual. An older couple, who didn't look Argentine, kept studying her intensely. Finally, Ruth's mother took her by the arm to introduce her to her friends.

"Hello, Inés," said the woman. "We're old friends of the family from Buenos Aires. We've heard very good things about you, that you're Ruth's high school classmate and a very good student. Have you ever been to the capital?"

"No, ma'am, I only know Corrientes. I live here by myself now, since my father passed away."

"How do you get along with older people and those who don't speak Spanish well?"

"I love older people like my grandmother and her sisters. And because of Ruth I'm used to being around European immigrants."

"Well, how would you like to come to Buenos Aires as a companion to an elderly lady from Russia? She needs help with the shopping and a little bit of housecleaning and, most of all, she needs company so that she's not alone while her husband works. They are very trustworthy, nice people. Ruth's parents have vouched for you because they know you well. The husband and wife have room for another person, so you would be very comfortable. They can give you room and board, plus a small salary so you can save, or send money to your mother if she needs it. If she agrees, we could take you with us by car a few days from now, when we're done with our excursions here.

What do you think?"

Inés looked at the woman in amazement, bewildered by this unbelievable possibility of escape. If her mother let her go, she would accept immediately. She would only regret leaving her on her own, and being away from her best friend, but she thought she could adapt to this unexpected adventure. She immediately ran to tell Itatí, who had no choice but to sadly agree though she was full of hope for her daughter. A few days later, Inés left to start her new life in the capital in the southern part of the country, a part she did not know.

***

The day I met her, I was on my way from high school to have lunch at my grandmother's house. My grandmother had promised me veal milanesas, but she had not told me that I would be sharing them with a stranger. At the top of the stairs, in the small entrance courtyard in front of the tiny kitchen, I met a young girl about my age who watched me with curiosity. She already knew a few things about me, but I'd had no idea she even existed. Her first words astonished me as much as her presence there:

"*Maité, Armando, mbá eichapá?*"

"Hello. Excuse me, but I don't understand a word you're saying. Are you here on a visit?"

"My apologies. I greeted you in Guaraní out of habit. I'm Inés, Mrs. Lita's new companion. I'm going to live with your grandparents. Nice to meet you!"

That day she was allowed to sit with us, but she usually ate in the kitchen while my grandparents and other relatives were in the living room. Her constant presence disconcerted me, but I wasn't afraid she was going to replace me in my grandparents' unconditional affections. I never got to know her well, because I soon started medical school, where I studied for six years, and so I had few opportunities to visit during the day.

I knew that they got along well, that she was kind and helpful and gradually became an invaluable companion to Lita, especially after my grandfather passed away a few years later. She also got along well with my cousin Patricia, who was a few years younger, and they spent a lot of time together. I had little contact with Inés partly because my college friends and I shared different interests. Also, I had my first girlfriend, so I had less time to spend with my family. When I finished my medical internship, I left the country to live and study in the United States. That was the last time I saw the young girl from Corrientes for the next fifty years!

Now, a lifetime later and in Seattle, my favorite city, memories that crept into my unconscious without my realizing it have resurfaced as if by chance.

As it happens, a few days ago Patricia called me on WhatsApp from Buenos Aires to wish me a happy birthday.

"How nice to catch you on your birthday, cousin! There are only a few of us left here to call you. My brother and his wife send a hug, and someone I just talked to on the phone sends a big greeting. Do you remember Inés, Lita's companion? When we spoke a little while ago, she insisted I say hello to you. She wants to know if you still like fishing, and if you use the method she showed you."

The reference to fishing gave me goose bumps. It brought back a summer's day when it was 35 degrees in the shade. It was the first time I participated in a fishing contest at the Costanera del Río de la Plata. I had no experience and no tackle, except for the gear Inés put together for me. She was knowledgeable in the ways of Corrientes, having spent her youth on the Paraná River with her family of fishermen and her dad, Gigí.

"Let's go to the hardware store to buy a nylon line, a silver spoon, a light sinker, and a hook. The rest we have in the kitchen," she said to me. She opened a can of peaches in syrup and emptied it out. Then she made a small hole with a nail, threaded the line through, and tied it to a small stick on the inside. "You'll win the championship with this because you'll catch more catfish than anyone else. I'll show you how to do it when we get to the river."

Her skill immediately became very apparent, because she could flip and throw the hook farther than many of the others on the waterfront. Within minutes I'd landed my first catfish with the same primitive technique! I didn't win the championship, but I had a lot of fun, and I still use the technique to this day. It helped me catch a tasty salmon that weighed several pounds while I was fishing from my kayak in the cold waters of British Columbia—to the amazement of the well-equipped Canadians watching in disbelief as I used my lowly technique from Corrientes!

A few days later I reached out again to Patricia who, in the meantime, had recalled other things that had happened.

"I also remember things we used to do together," she told me, somewhat excitedly. "In the afternoons we liked to sit with Inés in the little kitchen to listen to soap operas on the galena radio."

"The galena radio? I don't believe it! That was too much of an antique for anyone to use. By that time we already had good electronic equipment and television."

"We did, but they wouldn't let us use the stereo and the turntable in the dining room. Grandpa Lito brought the galena radio when he arrived from Palestine and somehow it was still in the kitchen. It played very softly and only tuned to one or two stations. You had to move the needle on the galena crystal to find a program. But we could also listen to a folk program that she loved, because sometimes they played music from Corrientes and tango, which she liked very much. Now one of her sons likes that music too."

"Wasn't she allowed to go out with friends on weekends?" I asked out of curiosity.

"Of course, as she grew up she went out with other girls from the neighborhood to dance in Palermo, in a place that played a lot of *chamamé*, and that brought back memories of her native province. That's how she met her future husband, an Italian from the south with whom she had two sons. You won't believe it! She named one Enrique, after your grandpa, and the other Marcelo, after your father, whom she was very fond of because he treated her like a daughter. I hardly see Inés now. She's quite old and doesn't visit or call us much. I wouldn't know how to get you to talk to her. But I heard that Marcelo is a well-known tango singer."

"That I'm interested in! As you know, tango is one of my passions. I'd like to get a hold of him. Maybe he can put us in touch with his mother. Do you know how to find him?"

"I can only tell you that his professional name is Facundo Catania."

"I'm going to search for him and see if he can help. I'd like to write about Inés's life before she moved to the capital, since I only know what the friends who brought her to our grandparents' house told me. They had talked a lot with the family who recommended her. But I would like to find out more about her indigenous background and her Sicilian father in Corrientes. At first, Inés would get confused and sometimes speak in Guaraní. At that time I was busy with other things and I wasn't at all interested in finding out more details. But now that I'm writing, it would be fascinating to know something about her life
before we met."

Nowadays it is very difficult to hide without leaving a trace, either from the police, or private investigators, or simply from the algorithms of major social media. It was not the first time that I unexpectedly found people on the internet and then used them as characters in one of my stories. This time, after a few minutes of searching, I discovered an ad for a tango show at the Homero Manzi Café, on the corner of Boedo and San Juan, two blocks from my grandparents' old home. The singer of the group was a certain Facundo Catania and he had a Facebook page and a contact number on WhatsApp. He got back to me immediately.

"Are you calling from the United States?"

"Yes, that's right. My name is Armando and I've known your mother, Inés, since we were young, when she lived at my grandparents' house. I haven't seen her since leaving the country fifty years ago. I wish I could talk to her about old times."

"Of course I know who you are. My brother and I know your family very well, the people my mother loved so much, and we knew your parents especially. They were so good to her. I can't believe it! I must call Inés and tell her! Wait, let's do this instead: I'll go see her right away at her nursing home nearby and let her talk to you on my phone, so you can speak directly. Expect a call from me in fifteen minutes."

A bit later the phone rang, and I talked to Inés as if fifty years were nothing, to paraphrase the lyrics of the tango, "Volver."

"Armando, I can't believe we're actually talking, and you still remember me. It's good that you had a little chat with my son, Marcelo, whose name is the same as your dad's. I miss your parents and grandparents so much. I still remember when you used to come by for lunch from school or college. Your grandmother used to make your favorite dishes, which I learned to make too. Can you believe that to this day I can still make *prakas*, the cabbage rolls stuffed with minced meat, and potato latkes, which my children also love? And I must be the only one from Corrientes who knows how to make a great gefilte fish and who understands Yiddish words." Strangely, as she was describing her abilities with Jewish cooking, I could hear music in the background that was indisputably a *chamamé*.

"Well, I'm still married to Diana, whom you met. We have a son who's a doctor like us and two grandchildren. But you will be even more pleased to know that I still fish with a can, just as you taught me when I was a student. You were right when you said you seem to have better luck with a can of peaches than any other fruit. Inés, I would like you to tell me something about your life before coming to the capital, when you lived in Corrientes and spoke Guaraní like your family. Do you remember back then?"

"I don't want to talk about that, and my children don't know those details either. All that's done with, and I don't remember a single word that's not Spanish. But now fishing comes to mind, just like you said. I was good at that. Let's talk about my life now. My husband and I ran a haberdashery until recently. He's Italian, just like my father, Gigí. Our children are Italian-Argentines, like many people around here, and Marcelo, well, Facundo as he now likes to be called, is a very popular tango singer. He has a show in your grandparents' neighborhood, where I also grew up. But I can't talk too much right now. I get tired, so I'd better pass the phone back to him. He'll tell you more. Better if you call back another day. A hug, and I hope you visit us soon."

It was nice to hear her voice and reminisce a bit, although I was very disappointed that she didn't remember, or didn't want to go into detail, about her youth while Marcelo was there. Nor had she revealed much to her children, who possibly were more familiar with Jewish than Corrientes food. It was obvious that life had been very hard in those days and that she had wanted to leave it behind. My options for gathering more data had suddenly fallen apart. It seemed clear that I wasn't going to find out more details and that her youth would disappear behind a cloud of mystery.

Marcelo acknowledged as much when he got back on the phone:

"Mom is a very good cook, and many of her recipes she learned from your grandmother, Lita. The strange thing is that now she doesn't feel like eating fish. I don't know if it's because the fish you buy here in the capital isn't always as fresh as she likes it, or because she doesn't want to remember some things she never told us."

"Marcelo, or Facundo if you prefer," I said, "I'm going to have to say goodbye for the moment. You and I share that I knew your mother when I was young, and besides that, I'm an old *milonguero* and as passionate about tango as you are. So I would like to listen to your music. Could you please send it as an attachment?”

"Absolutely. I'll send you my best hits. Then you can give me your opinion.”

"When we were talking to Inés, there was music playing in the background that sounded familiar. She says she doesn't remember her youth in Corrientes, but what she was listening to was a *chamamé*. It is clear that she still likes it. Well, Facundo, let's stay in touch, and either I'll visit you one day in Buenos Aires, or better yet, maybe we can arrange for you to visit the United States and sing at one of our milongas in Seattle. In the meantime, a hug for both of you!

Curiously, my rediscovery of Corrientes, its people, and its music proved to be prophetic. In proofreading this manuscript, Lupe, the editor of these stories in Spanish who lives in Madrid, sent me some comments that I want to share now:

"Dear Armando:

I don't know if I have ever told you that I am a great lover of South American music and I really like the accordion player, Chango Spasiuk. Surely you know him. Not long ago he came to play in Madrid. Alejandro, my partner, went to see him. I'm sending you a video about him in which he says that in 2020 UNESCO declared *chamamé* an Intangible Cultural Heritage of Humanity. I also thrill to *chamamé*."

VOODOO

The social distancing and lockdowns of 2020 have turned previously outgoing people into the 'newly awkward.' Without the pleasures of urban life and its chance encounters on the street, we have become rusty conversationalists. But I myself have welcomed the time for self-reflection. It has allowed me to resurface long-forgotten interests like my latent inclination towards superstition and magic. One lazy afternoon, I recalled the day I had resorted to voodoo to do bodily harm to an enemy.

Close friends who knew my predicament have wondered how it was possible for me, a thoughtful physician and critical researcher, to harbor dark thoughts and be prone to outlandish speculation. My interest in arcane topics such as spiritual philosophy developed during the 60s, when the journalist Louis Pauwels and the chemical engineer Jacques Bergier published *The Morning of the Magicians* in France. It became an international cult classic among the younger generation. Curiously, Bergier (born Yakov Mikhailovich Berger in Odessa, not far from my ancestors) was, like my uncle Nathan, a spy for the

French Resistance in Lyon. Bergier had been a Talmudic scholar of the Kabbalah and of forbidden history and occult studies. His background and interests drew me to his work. Yet, I understood from his author's statement that "there will be a lot of silliness in our book, but this matters little if the book stirs up a few vocations..." Certainly, this publication was influential in shaping my personality, and my interest in voodoo years later.

On a sleepless night during the pandemic, I recalled a casual encounter I had many years earlier while I was on vacation in Argentina, at the Atlantic beach resort of Mar del Plata. One afternoon, exhausted after a long walk, I felt an almost magnetic pull towards a particular bench in a city park. I had to share the bench with a stony elderly man, who looked me over with a gaze as penetrating as a bone X-ray. Then he turned to focus on the book I had on my lap and suddenly said:

"Are you a Jewish physician?

"Yes, I am. How did you guess?"

"I see things. And I know this book well. What made you read it?"

"I'm actually going over it for the second time because it's entertaining and pseudo-scientific. It covers a range of strange, unusual subjects that make it ideal vacation reading."

"You say it's entertaining, but I see you've gone over one chapter many times. Why are you fascinated by the theory of the coming evolutionary leap in human consciousness that will result in the new man?

Do you consider yourself one of the so-called mutations?"

"Of course not, that's pure speculation. But how do you know I'm reading this chapter? We've never met or talked before." I looked down at my closed book. There were no outward signs, like a bookmark, to indicate the section I was reading.

"I've told you, I'm clairvoyant. You bring to mind another Jewish doctor, one from the Middle Ages, who could predict the future. His name was Nostradamus. Have you heard of him?"

"Yes, I have. Nostradamus was French, like my father, and lived in St. Remy in Provence. I once visited his museum there. But serious research has debunked his prophesies. They're good fun but hocus-pocus."

"Don't be so skeptical. Why, then, are you reading this book?" As the subject of his inexplicable insight, I was growing more agitated by the minute. There was something mysterious, perhaps even evil, about the old man as if he were surrounded by a field of dark energy.

"How can you prove you are able to see things?"

"I don't need to prove it, but I can give you an example of this power. Just write down somebody's name on a piece of paper, fold it, and give it to me." I should have left, knowing that curiosity killed the cat. But somehow I couldn't pull away till I learned more about him. I scribbled the first thing that came to mind: the name of a close friend of my father with a tragic family history. The man took the paper from me, covered it with both hands, closed his eyes for a minute or so in order to concentrate deeply, and then said gravely:

"This is very troubling. It's blurred … but wait, I see something horrible. What is this? There's a small girl whose photo was in the newspapers years ago. What happened to her?"

His comment was terrifying! This man's faculties went beyond any previous experiences I'd had. By then, I was convinced of his capacity for clairvoyance.

"I don't know how you do it, but again you got it right. This man's little sister was the victim of a serial murderer. When he was caught, he was sent to the highest security prison in Ushuaia. How can you tell so much from a name I wrote down but one you didn't even read?" What he had just done was frightening and eerie. I stood up and turned to leave, determined to get away, but he reached out to stop me and made one final comment:

"I could sense you have similar powers as soon as you approached this bench, except you are not aware of them. You must learn to understand your own energy and how to harness it. In time, when you can control your mind, you'll find you can do other things. I predict that one day you'll be able to hurt an enemy just by wishing them harm. We are very much alike. Now go, and remember my words…"

I was horrified by his powers and the implications for my own future. I hurried away without looking back or planning to see him ever again. However, I consigned the encounter to some obscure corner of my subconscious mind.

My psychological defenses don't encourage me to think about that appalling meeting, but I was always aware of my proclivity to other morbid thoughts and fears. Once during a family trip to Bali some thirty years ago, my family and I sought refuge from a tropical storm inside a tea house. As was Balinese custom, the entrance gate faced the seaward, or sunset, side of the compound. My initial sense of foreboding was brought about by the sight of a bamboo screen behind the gate. It was there to force visitors to change direction by going around the screen and at the same time deter malevolent spirits from entering.

Diana, Serge and I were sharing a table with a group of young Dutch travelers on a bamboo-covered patio that had no walls but was open to the muddy road. Sunset and then darkness came suddenly as they do near the equator. We were then shrouded in a dramatic mist that the soft, romantic candlelight enhanced. The hypnotic sounds of a gamelan competed with the violent rain pummeling the vegetation outside. We chatted in hushed tones with our neighbors. The scene reminded me of an Edgar Alan Poe tale.

This nearly mystical moment was shattered by the unwelcome intrusion of a bat, the size of a small dog, that began to gyrate above our heads but stayed clear of the other travelers. The animal flew faster and faster in progressively tighter circles and barely missed our heads. I admit we were suburbanites unaccustomed to wild animals, small or large, in our immediate vicinity. Our dinner companions looked undaunted. Yet, the sensation was ominous. Why was it flying over our small group but avoiding the others? How could it see us so well in the weak candlelight? Was it a carnivorous bat that could have rabies?

Gripped by an uncontrollable fear, I threw some money on the table to pay the bill and we abandoned ship in disgrace, choosing instead to face the rainstorm on the pitch-black country road. Although the bat did not follow us, my apprehension persisted till we made it back to our lodge a mile down the road. As we walked away from the café, the rain slowly stopped, and the skies opened up almost unnaturally to reveal an infinite number of stars glittering in the blackest sky we had ever seen. Today, years later, our uncertainty in the face of the pandemic and our lack of control over an unpredictable situation have reawakened that feeling of dread before the unknown and the unforeseen.

I woke up the next morning with the premonition that the day would bring about an important change for the better and break the cycle of fearfulness. My perception was justified as it was followed by a propitious experience that would have pivotal consequences. We were thinking of taking a tour of the island after breakfast, one that focused on village life and provided photographic opportunities. I needed a driver and hoped to choose the best one among those hanging out, or napping, near the hotel. As I scanned the group, one of the drivers, a middle-aged, slender fellow with a peaceful expression, got out of his car and walked towards us. Almost simultaneously, as if by telepathy, we both made a clear choice. He had to be our chauffeur.

Once out in the countryside, we passed a rice farm and its house with yellow walls, surrounded by exuberant red flowers that were unfamiliar to me. Attracted by the colorful contrast, I asked the driver to stop so I could photograph the enchanting setting. I focused on a particular flower, letting the house blur into the background. The driver stood behind me, silently observing what I was doing. When I was done, he unexpectedly asked, diplomatically and in slow but educated English:

"Excuse me, sir. May I ask why you took this picture?"

"Sure," I answered, puzzled. "I live in a northern country with different vegetation and no tropical plants like these. I liked the strong color contrast between the flowers and the house."

"I see... But, excuse again, sir. Where is the human element"?

The question left me speechless. For the remainder of the tour, I replayed it in my mind at every photo opportunity. Next, we stopped at a village where two men were training their cocks for a fight. The driver asked them in Bahasa for their permission to take pictures, and I crouched down to their level so I could photograph the men, their expressions, as well as the fighting cocks. The men looked me over closely: I was as foreign to them as they were to me. The serenity of the village and the fierceness of the competing animals induced a surreal feel which I tried to capture in my images. The driver continued to observe me with interest but remained silent. When we returned to the hotel in the evening, I paid my bill and added a generous tip. Now it was my turn to question him:

"Your earlier question about my choice of subject was enlightening. How do you know so much about photography?"

He flashed a brilliant smile and without a word pulled a business card from his shirt pocket and proudly presented it to me. On it was his Indonesian name and his title: President, Balinese Photographic Society.

This unforgettable encounter determined the course of my future as a photographer. Ever since, before pressing the shutter, I remind myself of our driver's observation: "Where is the human element?" Now, many years later and frustrated by the social distancing forced on us by the pandemic, I can no longer act on Robert Capa's admonition: "If the image didn't work, you weren't close enough."

I usually carry a camera whenever I go out. On one occasion, while I was at work, this led me to confirm the proximity of an enemy. From the high vantage point of my office window at the hospital, I was admiring the sight of the trees below in the dense and mysterious fog. A motorcycle silently approached before fading into the patients parking lot. I took my camera to record the uncommon scene. My office door was open as usual. Suddenly I heard a familiar voice behind say sharply:

"I see you have time to play during working hours. So much for your complaints of being overwhelmed by too many clinical cases..."

The malicious comment was both loaded and unfair, since I was charged with the care of nearly a hundred patients. My colleague did not share this degree of responsibility and had plenty of time and freedom for her lab research. At the time, patient care and clinical research were far less rewarding academic careers in our medical school than lab investigation.

In spite of my difficult schedule, I struggled to work on lab research in the time available between patients. One of my funded projects had produced strong preliminary results, and I was very eager to pursue this area of study. It required radioisotope measurements and using a lab hood for proper venting. When I asked my colleague for permission to use the hood in the lab we shared, her response did not surprise me:

"Sorry, I cannot let you use the hood. As a clinician, you have less experience in the lab. You might contaminate the area, which would interfere with our own measurements. Find a hood somewhere else." The answer was ludicrous, as my assistant at the time was a biochemistry PhD who was highly competent in the lab. I was forced to find an alternative place and friendlier colleagues with decent dispositions.

Her antagonism was particularly fierce towards other women faculty who she thought might compete with her. She was a compulsive liar and an expert at inflating her own professional capacity. Thus, she had put herself forward as a candidate for president of the American Society of Women in Medicine—and she was nominated much to her surprise and my dismay.

My foe displayed her true colors again in a promotions committee meeting, when she voted against one of our younger faculty who clearly deserved advancement. However, our hypocritical colleague had already formed her own opinion:

"She's not ready to be promoted. Her research has been of moderate quality and not very imaginative. She is overworked with her patient care duties, and she has a family, two school children that need assistance, and a house to take care of. She has little chance of success in our difficult research field. Let's reconsider in the future."

But she had reserved her most stinging opposition to my own promotion, with severe repercussions for my career.

My dislike for her slowly turned to loathing. I needed no further proof. As Woody Allen said, "Just because you're paranoid doesn't mean they aren't out to get you." I just didn't know how best to take my revenge. I would have to pack a more powerful punch by enlisting obscure forces that were mightier than those available to her.

As it happened, I thought of a possible tool while listening to Afro-Pop—world music is one of my passions. So I learned that Haitian music could serve as an antidote to a flood of negativity. In 2010, Haiti was reeling from an earthquake, a cholera epidemic, and political disarray. In this context, a collective of musicians formed Lakou Mizik, a spectacular rhythmic band that mixed elements of Troubadour, Rara, and Rap. Eventually, the group incorporated the soulful spirit of church revivals and the trance-inducing intoxication of *Voudou* rituals.

Listening to Lakou Mizik under the influence of a powerful Haitian rum brought to mind the words of the clairvoyant I had met when in Argentina all those years ago. It was time to harness my mind against the forces of darkness. This sent me on a quest to understand the differences between voodoo practice and the *Voudou* (with a capital *V*) religion, which is more a way of life than a belief. The power of voodoo practices between 1791 and 1804 culminated in expelling the French from Haiti. The colonists who survived fled to New Orleans, taking with them French-speaking slaves who were voodoo practitioners. Both the *Voudou* religion and the magical practices of voodoo have survived in the fertile environment of New Orleans. And that city was my wife's next destination for a pediatrics conference!

I enlisted Diana's help in investigating the potential of Haitian practices as a defense against my evil colleague. Once she arrived, she sadly realized she would lack access to the authentic *Voudou* congregations where she could interact with established priests and priestesses, some of them initiated in Haiti. The casual visitor to New Orleans finds only sensationalist voodoo and ghost tours and "tourist voodoo" souvenir shops. However, in one of these establishments, the owner was an alleged 'doctor' or

'*Voudou* queen' who agreed to anoint one of the dolls with special powers during a ritual that she conducted right then and there. As an extra step, she advised that I should meditate under a sacred Mapou tree like the *Voudou* practitioners did when summoning sacred spirits.

When Diana came back home, I went as directed to the botanical gardens to sit under a Mapou. Afterwards, I opened the box Diana had given me and took out a pretty black figurine with a red dress and a headscarf. The simple instructions said: "Attach a few nail clippings or hair from the target person to the doll, and then prick the doll with pins wherever you want to inflict damage." In spite of the doll's doubtful origins, superstition got the better of me and I decided to give the ritual a try. I hoped I'd found the perfect revenge. My office was adjacent to that of my nemesis, so one night, while she was away at a conference, I collected some strands of hair from her couch. Then I pinned the strands in several places on the doll's legs before hanging it behind my office door in close proximity to my target. When the door was open, the doll could not be seen. I then directed all my mental energy to achieving my objective and confidently waited for the outcome.

I have to admit I was a little ashamed of my methods for settling old scores. I could hear my friends' skepticism—had they known what I was up to—echoing in my ear: "Did you expect this childish, superstitious trick to *work?*"

As it happened, exactly twenty-four hours after

my enemy returned to the office from her conference, she fell down the back stairs as she was going home in the evening and broke her right leg in several places. She couldn't move and had to wait in agony for hours till the maintenance staff found her. The orthopedic surgeon at the hospital had to implant large pins in her tibia, near to where I had stuck the pins on the doll!

I was very careful not to advertise that I had wished her harm and had chosen a voodoo doll as my instrument of revenge. Eventually, amazed by the spectacular outcome, I did discuss it with Marcel, my Haitian friend. He sneered at me and asked a predictable question: "How can you prove a 'cause-effect' relationship? Hard to believe you did any harm to the woman by fiddling with a doll." This same question had been nagging me for a long time, even as my coworker came to work with a limp and told the secretaries how little she was sleeping because of the pain. My feelings were mixed: I felt pleasure that I had succeeded yet slightly guilty over her discomfort.

Finally, after a year of seeing her suffer, I decided that justice had been done and my revenge was complete. With great satisfaction, I pulled the pins from the doll's leg and discarded them. The very next day, the woman's surgeon had a change of heart. He decided the surgical pin had much to do with her residual pain and it was time to remove it. Miraculously, and as conclusive proof of cause-effect associated with pulling the pins from the doll, my colleague has been pain free ever since. Better yet, she never suspected the sinister activities behind the door to the adjacent office.

A new side of this story concerns me more and more. My friend Marcel told me that sometimes the obscure forces of voodoo can turn back on a practitioner who is untrained in the dark arts of Haiti. These forces could sometimes return, with equal strength, to haunt the one who had commanded them. It is now 2020, long after my retirement from the hospital. This year my own left leg reached the final stage of osteoarthritis, and I needed a total knee replacement. Paradoxically, I now carry two thick titanium surgical pins on both the femur and the tibia. I have spent the whole year undergoing a slow, painful rehabilitation, wondering whether the forces I unleashed are now acting on my leg. Or maybe there's someone else practicing the obscure craft of voodoo on a doll that has my name?

SAUNA

The American yogi I had nicknamed "Naga Baba" walked naked and visibly shaken into the Athletic Club's sauna. He was alarmingly slim but muscular and, despite his anxiety, I could still detect a trace of his brilliant smile. His dark, penetrating eyes scanned the small space looking for his familiar, receptive audience, and then he burst out: "I nearly ran over a raccoon on Boren. What was he doing in this concrete jungle, with not a tree in sight? He was dodging the traffic, obviously terrified. And now I feel like the raccoon!"

I rushed to ask him for an explanation before he could start his usual meditation practice. It puzzled me that he would feel so agitated after his experience.

"I feel like the raccoon because I'm surrounded by aggression on all sides, and by political dysfunction and runaway technology. Don't you feel threatened by all the geeks coming to Seattle to work in hi-tech?" he asked, as if looking for emotional support. "The ones I fear the most are those pimple-faced young men and women who wear shorts even when it's freezing, the gamers who design software that's making a whole generation stupid." Then, still clearly shaken by his encounter, he added, "That's why this sauna is a sanctuary where I can practice my yoga, meditate, and chant the mantra I learned in India."

We all knew that he studied at a temple there for six months every year. He was single-minded in his goal: achieving *moksa* and stopping the eternal cycle of birth and rebirth.

After his tirade, he began to meditate and was lost to the world for some minutes. Across the bench, Gabriel—a compulsive reader from Colombia who was immersed in a Latin American novel—put a stop to his reading (a rare move for him) and looked at the yogi with curiosity.

"Excuse me, Arthur, maybe what I'm seeing is an optical illusion, because it's as dark in here as in a Thai nightclub. But it looks like there's an inch of space between your butt and the bench! Are you trying to levitate?"

Sitting in classical padmasana, with hips relaxed and legs crossed at an extreme angle (the culmination of years of practice), Naga Baba looked at Gabriel with a slight smile and responded thoughtfully:

"Expert yogis think that levitation is just showing off and that it doesn't help in their quest for liberation. I am an advanced yogi but not a sadhu. One of those holy men could be sitting here deep in meditation, and if he reached his goal, his spirit would leave his body to join a universal consciousness. I have tried for years to achieve *moksa* and free myself from being reborn into this material life, but, I have not reached that level yet. Very few do."

"Please, Arthur, don't do that to us!" Gabriel said, distressed by this possibility. "We'd be ecstatic if you achieved liberation, but it would be a shock to come into the sauna in the morning and find your empty body here. It might have dried up in the heat, or even begun to smell by then. Please try reaching *moksa* somewhere else, maybe in your temple in India next time you go."

As I witnessed this exchange in the sauna, I felt privileged to belong to this small group. The sauna was a microcosm of our city and its fascinating diversity. These thoughts were magnified by the arrival of my old friend Marcel, a muscular but nimble black Haitian who immediately began doing pushups, stretching and warming up his legs and low back, to get ready for his martial arts class. But he kept an eye on the now profusely sweating yogi. Marcel, a systems analyst, was equally familiar with the mysterious magic practices of his country. He had told us that Haitians were seventy percent Catholic, thirty percent Protestant, and one hundred percent Voodoo, now a recognized religion in his country. He was familiar with Naga Baba's beliefs. What surprised me now was seeing Marcel approach the yogi with an idea that might help him in his quest. "Arthur, did I ever tell you that I have my grandfather's recipe for a home-made potion of Haitian rum and other secret ingredients? He thinks it can have powerful psychological effects, and it may be just the catalyst you need to accelerate your progress towards moksha. Would you care to try some?" Naga Baba quickly agreed to try the family recipe.

"Excellent," said Marcel. "If it does the trick, then we'll celebrate by drinking some of it ourselves!"

At this point, Gabriel again stopped reading and removed his headphones so he could hear our conversation. He says he can listen to music or a pre-recorded podcast while simultaneously reading a book. He also claims he can split his mind into compartments like Napoleon was known to, read and listen at the same time, and never miss a word.

"Perhaps you could try voodoo as well, Marcel, and use those little black dolls they sell in New Orleans to stick pins into," I suggested flippantly.
The Haitian did not take kindly to this. "Get outta here, man! What does a retired medical researcher know about my country's religion?" he retorted, slightly offended by my encroaching on his turf.

With so many interruptions, Naga Baba was unable to meditate, but he smiled, and then scolded me:

"Pancho, you're a scientist! How can you be so superstitious and suggest we use unproven magic? This doesn't jibe with the guy I hear whistling Mozart tunes and Bizet's L'Arlésienne in the shower."

"Wait a minute, why did you call me 'Pancho'?"

"It's not a bad nickname, considering what you call me. You remind me of Pancho Villa, another stocky Latino with a huge untrimmed moustache who was very confrontational, like you. Only difference is he didn't wear cool Zero-G sunglasses. From now on,

I'm going to call you 'Pancho.'"

Marcel's idea of a potion sent me canvassing the sauna regulars on how to help the yogi reach his goal (even though he had never requested our assistance). I found Gabriel in the shower. At first, he didn't notice me and went on reading, holding his novel in his left hand, with his arm extended to keep the book from getting wet. This was no surprise to me since I had seen him swimming at the club. He would stop every few laps to read a page from a book he had left at one end of the pool. And he had recently appeared in the sauna with a bandage on his right shin. Apparently, he had been reading using a headlamp on the way home and had banged into a metal bar used for securing bicycles. A psychoanalyst friend of mine once suggested that I ask Gabriel: "What are you afraid you would think about if you stopped reading?"

Although Gabriel could not provide any insight for my project, he admitted feeling a little guilty about his earlier remark to the yogi. He asked me what I thought about his giving Arthur a present—his old edition of Siddhartha, the Herman Hesse book that had been a cult hit when he was an adolescent in Bogotá. I agreed that it would be a fine gesture.

On my way out of the club I met Pratik, another sauna regular and the yogi's unconditional admirer. He had been born in India and raised as a Hindu, but he claimed not to be much of a believer. Yet he hoped Naga Baba, with his deeper knowledge of the religion, might help him to "decipher the real meaning of the Dharma space." He also admired the yogi's human

side and his commitment to the "sacred" cow's wel-
fare; they had even visited a dairy farm together to observe the production process. He approved of Naga
Baba's trait of connecting the folks he liked with each
other—in fact, it had been the yogi who had introduced
Pratik and me in the sauna.

Regarding a way to help the yogi's spiritual development, Pratik was in favor of finding a technical
approach to understanding deep meditation. Yet, this
was not his area of expertise. He was interested in e-
commerce in emerging countries and wrote on global
economics and politics for the DailyO, an online plat-
form with a very large readership.

Later on that day, as I was daydreaming at my
favorite espresso bar, I thought of a way to image the
yogi's brain function as he advanced in his deep meditation practice. I decided to call on my friend Max, a
neuroscientist at the nearby Allen Institute of Brain
Science. He was always eager to show off his latest
accomplishment in mapping the human brain's neural networks. Max was a squash player and another
sauna regular, and he was aware of Naga Baba's practice and spiritual quest.

As soon as I entered Max's lab, I came face to
face with what seemed to be a live brain floating in the
center of the room. It displayed an extraordinary network of colored pathways that, to my untrained eye,
progressed in multiple directions in random order.
Max was using the latest in virtual reality equipment
and artificial intelligence software to map the inner
workings of the brain. He had managed to make these

instruments small enough to fit into a box the size of a smart phone.

I got straight to the point: "Max, this is fabulous work! Can you apply it to making an image of Naga Baba's brain as he reaches a deep stage of meditation? I've been watching him for a while now, and I think he may be getting closer to his goal. Could you catch him at the precise instant when he frees himself from this material life?"

"Are you serious, Armando? Sometimes I suspect you, Gabriel and Marcel are just old gossips." He sounded doubtful but did not fully reject my proposal. "This technology may well be the best there is for exploring this sort of thing. But we would have to be there when Arthur reaches the deepest level, to catch him with a spiritual 'smoking gun.' Listen, could you persuade him to become the subject of a study? He would need to come to my lab for a series of recording sessions and agree to be wired while he meditates." He paused, and then said, "In the meantime, could you bring me photos of him meditating from every possible angle? This will help in creating a working model for the images."

I had no trouble persuading the yogi to participate in this experiment, and he faithfully attended the sessions at the lab for several weeks. As soon as I could, I went to the locker room lugging my Leica cameras and a sturdy tripod to take a picture of him meditating on his wooden stool, which was now facing his favorite locker, No. 741. Arthur would already be deep in meditation, his skin shining from a generous application of coconut oil and the Ayurvedic cream he was so fond of. It was easy to catch him after his earlier meditation and hot yoga practice in the sauna, which he did twice every morning, and then again twice in the evening, for thirty minutes at a stretch. It was a grueling schedule that left him dehydrated and in desperate need of the two glasses of iced coconut water with lemon waiting for him in the locker room. He had fainted a couple of times after exceeding his thirty-minute limit and had once needed assistance when he had fallen and injured his head, which bled profusely. He was deeply ashamed of this experience. Because we were regulars at the gym, nobody questioned us about our photo shoot. I started taking his picture and soon he was as still as the Sphinx of Giza, his shallow breathing so slow that you could not be sure he was still alive. Several members passing by were stunned by this excessively slim, still character, and some even stopped for several seconds to observe him before walking away shaking their heads. Those of us who knew him better were wondering instead if he was really coming close to reaching his spiritual goal.

Later at the lab, Max seemed pleased with the high-resolution images I provided him with. For a serious scientist, he was curiously high-spirited and enthusiastic about my fanciful project. He then proposed we do a dry run at the club with the early imaging of Naga Baba's brain on a day he would not be there.

Max preferred not to influence the yogi's mind by showing him his own brain activity so early in the study. We agreed to do it soon.

A few days later, I learned that Naga Baba would be on vacation in Florida visiting his two grown-up sons, who were running in a race. Like their father, both were accomplished marathon runners. When I told Max, he suggested testing his instruments in the locker room at exactly six PM, when the club was busiest. We then told our closer sauna acquaintances they should try and be there for a visual presentation of the yogi's neural works.

When the time came, several of us drifted into the locker room not knowing exactly what to expect. To our great surprise, locker No. 741 was fully opened, with the bottle of coconut oil visible inside. Presumably, the yogi had changed his mind about attending the marathon in Florida, because there he was, sitting in a Lotus pose, facing the locker, and glistening with sweat after his evening sauna and yoga session. We watched him silently for a couple of minutes, not wishing to disturb his routine, and were struck by what appeared to be a gap between his body and the wooden stool. This gap seemed to be increasing by as much as one and then two inches in height! Could he really be levitating, despite his professed opposition to these "useless" feats?

Suddenly, an orange reddish, very thin, transparent flame could be seen surging from the top of his head for about a foot, vibrating slowly at first, then more forcefully, and turning a deeper shade of red. Our whole group was in a state of shock and incomprehension, more people were gathering behind us in complete silence, and someone had called the club manager to come watch the phenomenon.

Then, Naga Baba's body started to float upwards, maybe by as much as a foot, towards the ceiling, leaving empty space below. Abruptly, the red flame was gone, as if a light had been switched off. The yogi's body, still in padmasana, fell on the stool as if magnetized by the Earth. It remained immobile for a few seconds and then started to fade, until it completely disappeared, leaving the sad, empty stool behind. The only remaining sign of the yogi's presence was the strong scent of coconut oil we were all so familiar with.

Pandemonium broke out in the locker room. Everyone agreed that Naga Baba had finally achieved liberation and that he had done it here, at the club, among his friends. We were astonished to have witnessed the precise moment when a yogi achieved *moksa*. But it was unclear how he had managed not to leave his body behind for more than a few seconds, perhaps to spare us from having to dispose of the remains. Marcel was quietly shedding a tear, repeating softly what seemed like a mantra of his own: "My grandpa's rum syrup helped him! It really helped him!"

We all trooped out of the locker room in amazement, speculating wildly about this extraordinary event. Sadly, I realized that the yogi had not been wired at the time of his liberation. Now the world would never know what had taken place in his brain at the critical moment. On the other hand, I congratulated myself for having had the inspiration to ask Max for his scientific expertise. Perhaps we would still learn a lot from his meditation sessions. Maybe the powerful mental energy of all our friends had reached critical mass, which joined with the yogi's on his way towards spiritual liberation.

The entire Athletic Club was in turmoil, especially the sauna regulars, and everyone had a different theory about what had just happened. Someone called the newspapers, and the press were on their way to investigate. News of the incident had the potential of going viral, since no one in the West had ever been present when a yogi experienced *moksa*.

When I finally sat down with Max, away from the other members, I asked him for his opinion. What had happened was entirely different from what I had expected. I had been looking forward to a scientific presentation, and a preliminary view of the yogi's brain, like the one I had admired in his office, but I had witnessed a miracle instead!

Max pulled the small box I had seen in his lab from his pocket. He pointed at the miniature projector with the smug look of an alchemist who had discovered the philosopher's stone. Then he said:

"Don't take what you just saw at face value, Armando. Sometimes we hope so strongly for something to happen that we're willing to accept what we think we see as if it were real. The fact is, I was so impressed with the yogi's determination, and with his friends' ardent support, that I got carried away. And I was so eager to please, I took my idea of a dry run too far. The truth is all we saw was a hologram based on your photographs of the yogi meditating. I developed the images after researching ancient records of *moksa* cases in India."

"Wait a minute, Max. I'm very disappointed. This is so depressing! I'm a skeptical scientist like you, but all my life I've been seeking proof that one could transcend material life by spiritual practices. Finding evidence with my own eyes that illumination can happen during deep meditation was exhilarating. At least tell me: how advanced was he at the last session?" I was still determined to hear there had been tangible signs of the yogi's spiritual progress.

"Please don't take it so hard. And can you keep this secret for just a while longer? I was hoping to give you all a sense of the beauty of our Naga Baba reaching illumination. In fact, he never achieved a deeper level of meditation than at the sauna. But we'll continue with the sessions when he returns from his trip—though we may have to wait a long time before we can actually map his brain at the very instant he joins a universal consciousness.

"The hardest thing now will be to survive the indignation of our friends and club members when we explain and apologize for the stagecraft they just experienced. I hope they will forgive me for delivering only an optimistic illusion. But for now, let's slip out quietly before the press gets here, to find Gabriel and Marcel, and try out that mystical rum concoction. We deserve a reward for our dramatic hi-tech success. And then maybe I'll screw up enough courage to tell them what really happened."

We did survive the wrath of the club members but were not prepared for another outcome. After the hologram presentation, nobody saw the yogi again. He was absent from the lab sessions, and from the sauna, and the manager said he had stopped paying his monthly dues and had left town without explanation. Pratik was especially disappointed that he had run away like a thug and departed without honor. He felt the yogi had been stubborn and proud in refusing to carry his water bottle inside the sauna room and suspected that "his fainting and tripping, and his injuring himself at the sauna, had shamed him too much." Later, Pratik added that he was offended that "Arthur was a different person than he pretended to be in the sauna." He even disclosed the yogi had "actually tasted meat from other people's dinner plates since it was free, even though he claimed to be strictly vegetarian."

After a few months had gone by, Pratik discovered that the yogi had posted photos of himself in a new job as an extra in a Hollywood studio. Pratik was especially distressed that while Naga Baba "had always wanted to be perceived as following the Dharma, he was basically nothing more than a helpless, obsessive hippy."

And then he received an email from the yogi:

Pratik prabhu, my dear friend, most certainly from many previous lifetimes: Please tell my equally dear friend Armando that the racoon trapped and frightened in the middle of a very busy Seattle Street has now moved and is equally trapped and frightened in the jungle of the American film industry in Hollywood. Peace and love to all you, dear friends in Seattle.

NASTASSIA

The day Nastassia Vanholder-Lacroix underwent yet another spectacular transformation, her husband reached his breaking point. He cancelled a meeting with his customs broker—an unusual and dramatic move for him—and instead approached me, a trusted friend and established psychoanalyst, for help. When we met, Phil was nervously dipping a biscotto into his hot, foamy cappuccino when he suddenly exclaimed with alarm:

"Maurice, will you agree with me that magical realism is dead? It's clearly no match for the surreal complexities of our own lives!"

As usual, Philip's opening statement made no reference to his wife's bizarre behavior. Rather it reflected his perception of human existence as another dimension in a theoretical universe. Even now that I know the case better, I cannot decide whether his outburst was triggered by the demise of that popular trend in Latin American fiction or by his distress over his wife's metamorphosis. Certainly, his extreme literary judgment made sense in light of her inexplicable changes in appearance and behavior.

"Please, I need your help! You have the right background. You're a psychoanalyst, you're familiar with some of the esoteric doctrines of the Far East—" He suddenly stopped working on his hard biscotto, tried to sit back in a relaxed posture, but soon gave up.

By the time we met to chat, Nastassia's condition had stimulated the imagination of everyone in our group of inveterate foodies and espresso addicts in Seattle. Our kingdom was the cavernous, gloomy, wood-paneled room of Torrefazione Toscana, a coffee-roaster (and bit of heaven) in the eternally drizzly Pacific Northwest. It was the magnetic center that pulled our small expatriate community together. As hyper-critical, experienced observers, we shared the opinion that its aromatic espresso was roasted to perfection, smooth and flavorful with no unpleasant aftertaste, and certainly the most "Italian" in the city. They served it in decorated Florentine ceramic cups that made the experience complete.

Besides the quality of its coffee, the Torrefazione was a microcosm populated by the eclectic characters who circulated by its counter. There were architects, art gallery owners, homeless people in need of a warm cup of drip coffee, geeks from the newly developed software industry in the neighborhood, plus literary types in search of a stimulating venue for short-story writing. Although the café was usually peaceful, sometimes chaos and unpredictability ruled the day—but the unusual case of Nastassia Vanholder Lacroix was something else altogether. It had started with her theatrical arrival at the port of Seattle to a nearly full complement of café friends. Her gait, as she came down the Dutch freighter's ramp, was like a professional model's, and at the same time completely natural. It was obvious that the sight of his new bride filled my friend, Philip, with pride and admiration.

Philip (Phil) Good had married Nastassia in Holland, in an elaborate ceremony on a river barge moored on the Heerrengracht in Old Amsterdam. She was a highly paid haute couture designer at home on the Grand Boulevards in Paris, in London Town, or in the fashion houses of Milano. A dark, slender, eccentric beauty, she modeled her own creations for weeks before releasing them to the press. Unlike other designers, her impeccable taste was complemented by a rigorous technical training at the famous École des Beaux Arts in Paris and the Technological Institute in Prague. She favored exquisite textiles for long, kimono-like outfits inspired by the stoic samurai tradition in medieval Japan. She would wear the dark gray or indigo militaristic attire with a nonchalance that made it work equally well in an American supermarket or at one of her cocktail parties in Paris, which she frequently hosted in the Marais.

Phil had told me of their first, chance meeting during one of his frequent Nepalese treks. He had been searching for ancient Tibetan manuscripts to "import" by questionable means to the United States. He and Nastassia had crossed paths on a snowy field at 12,000 feet. The sight of the slender, kimono-clad woman who spoke with a Dutch accent, wore tasteful French perfume, and had European manners took his breath away. After marrying a few months later, Nastassia was on her way to Seattle, where our snooty café community received her with open arms. Her relationship with Phil went from strength to strength, and they soon became an enviable example of a well-matched, adventurous, attractive couple who could look forward to a loving future together.

Soon enough, we began to socialize, and one day I invited them for dinner. At her request, I served an "aromatic fish" casserole, a recipe adapted from Roy Andries de Groot, a famous British-born but very Dutch chef we both admired. I had taken some liberties with the dish. As de Groot himself had said: "The perfect marriage of food and wine should allow for infidelity."

During dinner, Nastassia suddenly asked, "Maurice, would you play some music to match your delicious meal?" I turned on my record player and chose a Mozart piano sonata played by Lili Kraus, a renowned interpreter of Mozart and Beethoven. I expected that Nastassia would appreciate her rendition but was not prepared for the suddenness of her reaction. At the first few notes of the sonata, she broke into loud, convulsive sobbing, weeping uncontrollably and covering her face with both hands.

I turned the music off at once and went back to the table to find out what was happening.

"Don't be alarmed, Maurice," Phil said to calm things down. "Nastassia is extremely sensitive to Mozart's music. She loves it, but at the same time it brings up memories and strong feelings."

When Nastassia recovered, she apologized: "Thank you, Maurice. Sorry about the drama. I am very fond of Mozart, but it's too much for me. I can't avoid feeling a deep sadness when I hear his music. Please, play something else, anything else."

I should have guessed that Nastassia's hypersensitivity might be an indication of the episodes to come. None of us who frequented the café had expected to be immersed, just a few months after her arrival, in heated discussions regarding the causes and implications of Nastassia's suddenly outlandish behavior, which prompted Phil to request my assistance.

* * *

Several days after he first approached me, we met up again to discuss the situation over coffee. The first thing Phil said was: "Do you remember Zelig, the Woody Allen character who transmutes himself like a chameleon? He could adopt the external appearance, as well as the psychology and behavior, of the people around him. I believe that Nastassia has been affected by a similar syndrome. I can find no other rational explanation."

"Have you talked to her? Is she aware of her

transformations and other people's reaction to them?"

"At the start, she dismissed everyone's concerns attributing the changes to her own original style. With her inimitable accent and peculiar English phrasing, she told me she's just responding to the "boreness" of her new life in America. Maybe this ennui is the root cause of her repeated transformations.

"Her first episode happened during a recent visit to London," Phil continued. "While exploring South Kensington, we found a traditional Indian restaurant, the Kerala Spice Trail, where we stopped for a delicious, romantic meal. We finished it off with fresh fruit just in from India. She described the dessert as the best mango she had ever tasted but then became strangely introspective. After lunch, we separated for a few hours. I went to visit a Chinese antiques merchant I knew. He was thinking of selling a Cambodian Buddha allegedly smuggled by Andre Malraux during one of his early trips to Angkor. Meantime, Nastassia went strolling on her own with no particular destination in mind. We both returned to the hotel at 8 PM, entering through the revolving door and heading towards the elevator at the same time. Can you believe I didn't recognize her at first? She was dressed in a colorful Indian sari, had a purple dot painted on her forehead, and exuded a curious scent redolent of cardamom and cumin. More inexplicably, she no longer spoke with her usual Amsterdamer accent but pronounced her English like a Keralan!"

"Were her appearance and behavior temporary, or did they become permanent traits?"

"This phase, or should I say phenomenon, lasted for days. She was otherwise normal, but had adopted the appearance, style, and psychology of an elegant Indian woman. You may remember, when we returned to the United States she remained in this guise for a while, awakening everyone's curiosity. We all initially attributed this behavior to her eccentricity, but it soon became clear that we were mistaken because she transformed again, this time into—"

"Wait, Phil! Did anything facilitate her next change in appearance?"

"Maybe you have a point there. One afternoon we came across a woman friend, an avid body builder and marathon runner, you know, like the ones you see around Seattle, especially near the university campus or by the lakeside. She offered Nastassia a bite of her Power Bar, which she apparently ate every day for lunch with nuts and berries, and a swallow of her Power Jock Juice. The next evening I arrived home to find Nastassia attired in electric blue Lycra pants and a T-shirt, and sporting a short, masculine hairstyle. Gone were the Indian perfume, the Keralan accent, the sari, and she greeted me with an expression she had never used before: 'Hey, man, give me five!' Her accent was now totally Northwest! Curiously, in the next few days she seemed to become more muscular, developing a tremendous resistance to fatigue. In fact, she joined in a 10-kilometer race and finished alongside the fastest runners, although she had never exercised regularly in the past. I must confess I didn't like her new appearance or less refined manners."

"For sure, these changes are amazing, but so far I see no clear explanation for them."

I wondered, without saying so, if she had participated in a religious or tantric ritual or taken part in rebirthing sessions, which allegedly can revive memories of past lives or incarnations. I was at a loss as to how I might help. I needed more information, which he gave me willingly.

"Was she using any illegal substances?"

"None at all. But there may be other triggers that bring about her changes at short notice. Like when we celebrated a friend's birthday at Shanghai Gates, a particularly good Chinese restaurant in the International District. The long beans in preserved shrimp (imported from China) and the variety of mushrooms were exceptional. Because I experienced vivid dreams later that night, I wondered whether a psychedelic mushroom might have contaminated the wonderful dinner. Predictably, by the next afternoon Nastassia had adopted the regal appearance of a Mandarin dowager or a madam in a pre-war Shanghai bordello. Her normally dark hair had become pitch black, while her eyes had taken on an unmistakably Asian shape. Her long, flowing Chinese silk robe wrapped itself around her body as if she had been born to wear it."

Phil was obviously at his wit's end. I knew he had stopped playing squash at the gym, had not been seen in any of the art galleries where he hunted for Asian antiques or forgotten manuscripts, and had otherwise avoided most of his acquaintances.

"Her changes have become intolerable to both of us. She is now aware that I dislike these transformations. And she's also worried that people are avoiding her, frowning at us, or openly turning away when she arrives as if uncertain of what she might do next. She wishes these changes would stop. I hope you can help us!" He was certainly showing signs of severe distress, dropping his biscotto, then picking it up, only to discard it after a cursory look. He added more sugar to his cappuccino and then made a face at its unacceptable sweetness. Then he proceeded in fits and starts to describe the latest turn of events:

"Let me tell you about our recent trip to visit distant relatives in Muskogee, Oklahoma. (You know I'm not too thrilled about this very conservative family connection.). While 'over yonder' we attended the famous Rattlesnake Hunt Festival. The dexterity of the town's butcher was mesmerizing. Hunters of all ages brought their catch to the competition, since there were prizes for the biggest and the smallest snake and for the most poisonous one too. Like everyone else, we tasted a rattlesnake sandwich, which isn't too different from one made with chicken or rabbit. As I sadly anticipated (without admitting this to my friends, partly out of shame) ever since that day Nastassia has been wearing blue jeans, which she never did in the past—Lee's Western style, to be precise—a checked shirt, and lizard-skin boots. A mysterious blond ponytail has replaced her previous Dowager Empress style coiffure. Our house is now shaken by the shrill music of Woody Guthrie, and she is eating grits for breakfast, for heaven's sake! I have also found a suspicious package in our freezer, containing some elongated chunks of white meat ... though I can guess where it comes from," he concluded. By now his skin was sweaty and his pupils alarmingly dilated as though he were having a panic attack.

"Please calm down, Phil. I'll do what I can to help you both. Of course, I could try hypnosis if she would let me. That's what Mia Farrow, Woody's psychiatrist in the movie you mentioned earlier, did. But I'm starting to develop a reasonable theory, which is less esoteric than you might wish. Ideally, I would like to interview Nastassia in person, but I suspect she may not agree to that either. Her puzzling metamorphosis reminds me of the writings of G.K. Chesterton, of Father Brown's detective series fame. Have you read his Christian mysteries, or The Man Who Knew Too Much? He suggested that 'there usually is a rational explanation to otherwise inexplicable or apparently supernatural events.' Following this line of thought, we may be dealing with a paradox rather than a miracle. If we accept that an event or a mystery may have occurred in any of multiple universes or space dimensions, it follows that there must also exist infinite solutions, one of which may explain the facts in their entirety." I was conscious of my pseudo-scientific tone, but I could not help feeling self-important. Somehow, I had to be helpful, come up with a practical approach, something reasonable and down to earth.

"I think that the external trigger for all these

events is a gustatory stimulus, possibly the ingestion of certain foods which may reawaken her inexhaustible 'memory of taste.' For instance, that delicious mango in the Kerala restaurant must have sparked a powerful recollection, which then resurfaced as a genetic archetype in the shape of a quintessential Indian woman. The mango must have transported her to the space-time in which one of her Vanholder-Lacroix ancestors, perhaps merchants in the infamous Dutch East Indian Company, may have coupled with a Keralan beauty, with profound unpredictable effects in future generations."

"I like this idea! But I'm skeptical by nature. Assuming your theory is right, can you provide an antidote? Can you restore her to the Dutch designer she once was?" He had stopped sampling the foam on his cup and was observing me closely, hopeful for a solution to his wife's misfortunes. My reputation as an infallible diagnostician was at stake, yet I elaborated further, perhaps digging my own grave:

"The treatment I would like to propose entails creating strong associations to revive her experience of growing up in Holland. Tracking down the necessary staples will require both ingenuity and your networking resources. You must obtain as soon as possible, by legal means or not, a large supply of certain foods that may be hard to find in Seattle," I said. I was still unsure I was on the right track.

"Don't worry, I can do this! I will ask Nastassia about the food she ate as a child. I'll also call her mother in Amsterdam to gain her perspective on what

Nastassia liked to eat when she was very young, which she might not recall on her own."

"That's the attitude, Phil! The key will be to identify these items and give them to her in small amounts, at regular intervals, especially before and after your incursions into ethnic restaurants, in particular when you're travelling abroad. This program is analogous to carrying a snake-bite kit, or a bee-sting emergency syringe with epinephrine for people who are allergic to these poisons," I said with more confidence than was prudent in such an unusual case.

During the following weeks I was fretful, awaiting news from my friends. I called Phil occasionally on the phone to get reports about Nastassia's progress, but he seemed a little reticent about giving me any information. Finally, we met again at our usual café, the Torrefazione Toscana.

"Maurice, I'm so grateful to you! It was a great idea to consult you about Nastassia's mysterious transformations. Can you believe she is responding just as you thought she would? She has turned back into the dark, tasteful Dutch designer, the one that I fell in love with at first sight in the Himalayas."

"What did you do to achieve these excellent results?"

"First, we talked for a long time about Nastassia's childhood in Holland. Then, I sent her mother several emails asking for her recollection of what her daughter ate back then. Somehow, I developed a tactical plan for the management of what you called her 'gustatory-triggered metamorphosis.' My first idea was to keep a permanent supply of that most fragrant of Dutch cheeses, like the Overjarige Boeren Kaas that Nastassia loves and cannot be without. Similarly, I used my art import connections to find an excellent source for weekly airmail deliveries of kippered herring and smoked eel, which I knew Nastassia would associate with her visits to North Sea resorts or her summer home in Volendam. For good measure, we added some common Edam cheese from the same district, although this may have been less effective than the aged, pungent cheese I mentioned earlier."

"Did you use other foodstuffs to bring up any associations from when she was very young?"

"Yes. I thought of something very effective. Are you familiar with Advokaat, that sweet, egg-based alcoholic drink? It's often used to placate young children in the Netherlands. I gave it to her at the beginning of her rehabilitation when I felt it might be most effective. We still keep doses in the medicine cabinet and in both of our cars, and I plan to give her a full dose at the slightest premonition of a gustatory flare-up. Finally, I introduced an element that you didn't suggest. In a stroke of imagination, or maybe intuition, I added a visual cue to her surroundings, which was of benefit to both of us. I can tell you, in confidence, that I obtained a rare (maybe even counterfeit) Vermeer painting of a beautiful young woman wearing only a pearl necklace which Nastassia has found curiously erotic and stimulating!"

The strongest evidence that she has fully recovered is that Nastassia travelled on her own to

Cambodia, originally to buy silk for her designs. In Phnom Penh she heard of a village of silk makers, and hired a motorcycle driver to take her there, negotiating the dangerous, mine-infested country roads. She met with a remarkable group of village women who produced wonderful silk in classical, intricate patterns, but had no outlet for selling it. Nastassia has proposed a system of micro-loans to help the village expand its business. She hopes the women can go on to produce silk in much larger volume, sell it to her at a profitable, yet competitive cost, and maybe even learn haute couture techniques.

Phil and Nastassia have come back to our coffee group at the Torrefazione. She appears as elegant and radiant as ever, and calm has been restored to the reunions now that we are reassured of her mental health. She has adjusted to her life here and no longer complains of "boreness" in America. For my part, I feel highly rewarded by her recovery. As an unexpected benefit, I'm now receiving consults concerning other unusual situations from different members of our coffee community.

This story was imagined in 1993, New Year's Eve, and revised during the 2020 pandemic, as a survivalist project.

THE MAN WHO LEARNED TO LOVE THE BOMB

Mr. G. walked into my office slowly, perhaps because of shyness or even mistrust. He wore a brown tweed jacket that was a little threadbare, a white shirt in need of ironing, and a striped tie from some English regiment. I guessed he could be a high-school teacher. He introduced himself indifferently, sat down opposite me, and explained that he had high blood pressure. His general practitioner had recommended that he consult a specialist because his previous treatment had been unsuccessful. "This looks like a routine case involving someone who isn't particularly interesting," I thought to myself. But as often happens with my first impressions, I was doubly wrong.

He told me that he was a retired widower and he was a bit bored. In contrast to his previous life, his current situation gave him little motivation for staying active. Also, for a couple of months now he had been bothered by intermittent abdominal pains. I checked him over carefully and thought I could feel a deep, expanding pulse behind his navel.

"Mr. G., what job did you do?"

"I'm an army veteran and demolitions expert. During the Korean War, they called me up to work in sabotage against the Northern troops. I destroyed bridges over the Yalu and Han Rivers as a way of deterring enemy incursions into South Korea. I was lucky not to have injuries or accidents, and I gradually got used to the risks. After leaving the army, I spent many years applying my experience to civilian construction work, and working in mines and quarries, up until retiring recently. And since then, I've been downhearted, with no interest in anything, and I sleep poorly."

"I'm sorry to hear that, and I'd like to help you. I want to monitor your blood pressure and evaluate those stomach pains you've mentioned. First, let's discuss your diet. I'm going to suggest a diet called "DASH," which consists of fresh foods, especially fruits and vegetables, and no processed or canned products. I need to make a few changes to your medication, and I'm going to order an abdominal ultrasound. It is a noninvasive exam and not at all bothersome."

He said goodbye somewhat more cheerfully and promised to look after himself a little.

When he returned to the clinic three weeks later, his blood pressure had dropped to almost normal. He appeared less downcast and, though he was dressed the same, he was not wearing a tie. He wanted to know the results of the tests.

"You look better to me, Mr. G. But, the ultrasound surprised us. We discovered that a part of the abdominal aorta is somewhat dilated—something we call an aneurysm. It's only three or four centimeters in diameter, so it's not serious, but it could be what's causing the pain. We should repeat the test every six months to see if there are any changes. Also, let's add a beta blocker to reduce the pulse pressure on the aneurysm. This medication can make you a bit weaker, but that's all. I recommend reducing your physical activity to minimize any risk—no running or jumping, for example."

As I went over the details, he appeared more anxious. He swung his leg over the opposite knee, and his hands trembled a little.

"Tell me, Doctor, how dangerous is this aneurysm?"

"Please don't be alarmed. For now, we just have to be watchful. Many aneurysms remain stable and without any complications, but if yours increases in diameter quickly, that would be worrying. If that happens, there's a possibility of a spontaneous rupture. I think that with treatment we will be able to monitor it successfully and watch how it progresses."

"Do you realize, Doctor, that I'm an explosives expert, and I now have a bomb in my own body? I'm going to find it difficult to adapt to this. I've never been afraid of bombs, but I'm carrying this one inside me! On the one hand, you're suggesting I should take better care of myself and avoid overreacting and doing anything risky. But on the other, I should live more intensely and take advantage of every moment. I will have to learn how to manage both options."

As he was leaving, he moved somewhat uncertainly towards the door; he was so lost in thought that he forgot to say goodbye or look back.

Soon his blood pressure was under control and he had lost a few pounds. However, the aneurysm continued to grow, to about five centimeters in diameter. I was aware that Mr. G. was wrestling with a dilemma, with two contradictory situations. I felt obliged to warn him again and recommend he led a calm and quiet life. I wondered how he would strike a balance between the two opposing choices facing him.

After learning about the implacable growth of the aneurysm, Mr. G. continued to transform both his appearance and personality; this was as obvious as the melting of glaciers in Greenland. He swapped his professorial tweed jacket for a leather aviator jacket, which he wore over a colorful check shirt and blue jeans that seemed to me too close fitting for his age. He strolled around, almost defiantly, in caiman-skin boots, which were unusual in the United States.

His eyes shone more brightly than I remembered from his first visit, and he seemed happy with himself.

"Doctor," he said unexpectedly, "have you been watching the news on television? Like everyone else, you must have heard about my news. It was a real show, and I am proud of the outcome. No one was hurt and the houses around remained intact."

"Sorry, Mr. G., but I don't know what you are referring to. I see you're very excited. Tell me what's going on."

"The demolition of the Kingdome, the huge baseball stadium with its capacity to hold 80,000 people! It's been my most important project since the end of the war. My former boss got them to call me so I could oversee the project. We had to produce an implosion, with explosives strategically placed to prevent damage to the neighborhood and to protect the surrounding buildings and barracks."

"Congratulations on carrying it out successfully! It was amazing. I saw it on the news, but it never occurred to me it was your doing. However, now I'm concerned you have such an active job—it's certainly not prudent for someone with a growing aneurysm."

"My assistants did the hardest part. But at the same time it was a great personal experience, and in a way it's brought me back to life. I sleep better now and wake up feeling rested. Being idle affected me very negatively. Changing how I spend my time and regaining my self-esteem seem to me more important than the risk posed by the aneurysm, because I'm used to bombs and explosions. But the emptiness and lack of objectives were intolerable."

A few weeks went by, and one morning I received a call from a member of his family:

"Doctor, it's Laura here, Mr. G.'s daughter. I need to tell you that my father has changed a lot since he was diagnosed with what he calls "my inner bomb." He's become very irresponsible and isn't following through with his treatment. Every day he does something reckless, and this alarms us. I'm calling you because he's surprised us with another bit of craziness. He's joined a skydiving club, something he has never done before. He says he's training for his first jump in the next few days. At his age ... and with an aneurysm!"

Of course I tried to get hold of him, but he did not respond to my calls. Mr. G. was an adult and would have to live with the consequences.

He must have survived the jump, because he turned up in radiology for the ultrasound as planned. Unfortunately, the exam showed that the lesion had increased to a critical degree to more than six centimeters in diameter. I scheduled an appointment for him for soon afterwards.

"How are you, Doctor? I'm sorry my daughter's been bothering you. But as you can see, nothing bad happened to me. I made my first jump with no consequences except to my mental health, which continues to improve every day. It was an extraordinary adventure, an experience I've always wanted to have. But don't worry, my blood pressure is under control and I've had no side effects from the beta blockers as you'd feared."

"That's great, Mr. G.! I really admire your decision to skydive. I wouldn't dare do it myself. And I am pleased with the feat's positive effects. But I regret to inform you, because it's my duty, that the aneurysm has grown rapidly to more than six centimeters. This increases the risk of a rupture, which could be catastrophic, and surgery may soon be necessary. I suggest you start consulting with a vascular surgeon."

He thought for a long time before answering:

"Doctor, I prefer not to see a surgeon. I've read up on this a little and talked to friends. The operation is difficult, and I've been told that it has a high mortality rate. I'm already used to carrying my bomb inside, because it is my profession, and I'm handling it carefully and with years of experience. I prefer to leave it alone and instead enjoy life as I haven't done for a long time. Imagine, the army's technical core has once again asked me to give demolition courses to new cadets and also help with special projects! It's a well-calculated risk. You can see that my blood pressure is under control. I think it's better not to talk about surgery at the moment. Can't we continue with these visits, repeating the ultrasound as we've done up to now?"

"In these cases, the patient's decision is very important. Meanwhile, tell me, how are those stomach pains?'

"I'm glad to say a bit better, depending on what I've eaten."

"The discomfort could have other causes. Would you allow me to order more tests and a gastroenterology consult?"

"I'm sorry, Doctor, I'm already worried enough about the aneurysm. Let's see if the pains continue to bother me. I'm going to be very busy teaching, and I've also been offered a small job in some mines in Idaho, which I haven't accepted yet. If I travel and can't call you, my daughter Laura will get in touch with you. She's a geologist and thoroughly understands the methods we use in mining. She could keep you informed about my health and tell you about my activities."

Although today doctors are overwhelmed with administrative duties, receptionists and nurses insulate us from external calls. But I found Mr. G.'s case both worrying and astonishing. That's why I gave orders not to block Laura's calls, so I could know what my unusual patient was up to.

I soon learned that he had tired of teaching young cadets in a barracks and preferred to accept jobs that exposed him to greater risk but were more interesting. First, he took part in the demolition of large old buildings, which were to be replaced by masses of concrete and glass to accommodate newly arrived hi-tech workers for the expanding computing industry. Then he accepted a naval commission to study the harmful effects of underwater explosions on the whales in Puget Sound.

But Laura and I soon lost touch with him after he gave up renting his downtown apartment and moved to Coeur D'Alene, Idaho.

I tried to guess the reasons behind the radical change of address. The area, known for the presence of militant and extreme right-wing groups, was where the largest silver mines in the country were located. Although they had closed for several years because of the metal's fall in price, I read that one of them was going into production again. I then assumed that Mr. G. would not be far from that mine since a demolitions expert would be essential.

Laura's next call confirmed my suspicions and made me more anxious about my curious patient.

"Doctor, thank you very much for taking my calls. My father has agreed to work at the silver mine, an operation that would be risky for anyone but especially for someone with an aneurysm. It requires some physical effort even though he has several assistants he can rely on. The explosion itself is usually well controlled, but the preparations can also be dangerous."

"Do they use dynamite?" I asked innocently.

"Today, they use ANFO for deep excavations. It's a mixture of 94.5% ammonium nitrate and 5.5% diesel fuel. These substances are brought in separately by truck and then mixed at the last moment, and the granules are injected into pre-installed pipes using air compressors. The same mixture is used to prevent avalanches in areas where there is heavy snowfall.

"What would be the difference if they used ammonium nitrate fertilizer? I've read that it can explode spontaneously and is used by terrorists."

"Even without it being mixed with something else, this compound can deteriorate over time and self-detonate. though that's quite rare. Fortunately, ANFO is a tertiary explosive and requires a primary detonator plus a primer to make it explode. They used to use dynamite but nowadays they use Tovex or pentolite. The issue is that terrorists have learned to use these different combinations. In 1995, in Oklahoma, they used a compound called ANNM, which has nitromethane."

"Well, Laura, if I was worried about your father before, I feel even more anxious now. I understand that he's an expert, but in his case I think the risks are quite serious. Please keep in touch and tell me any news as soon as you have it."

A few days later, an article in the local newspaper caught my eye: "Idaho mine reopening canceled due to dangerous explosion." Several people had been wounded, some seriously, but they did not mention any names. I was very worried and asked our secretary to search out Laura so I could find out how her father was. For several days it was impossible to locate her, but then one morning she called me at the office.

"My apologies, Doctor, for not returning your calls before now, but I've been out of reach in Idaho. I'm sorry to be the bearer of bad news: my father has just died in the hospital in Coeur D'Alene."

"I'm so sorry! I was concerned since I heard about of the accident at the silver mine, although the paper never mentioned the names of the casualties."

"You won't believe this. My father was in a pretty bad way before the explosion at the mine, which he never took part in. He died of complications from colon cancer. He himself did not know about his condition until the last moment, before he slipped into a coma brought on by liver failure. But I can assure you that he never allowed the aneurysm to dishearten him. Instead, it helped him to live his last months with great intensity and a sense of purpose. I know you held him in high regard and were concerned about his health. I think we will both agree that he 'died with his boots on,' which is what he would have wanted."

BESSARABIA

Bessarabia, 1903

The primary school in the tiny and inconsequential village of Yawo had only one teacher and very few students. Fanny had started school at the age of six. Because she spoke Yiddish with her family, she complained of having few friends: the other children were Russian or Romanian and did not want to play with her. Many in the shtetl studied at home or in the small synagogue under the rabbi or cantor.

The Radovitskys, who were poor but learned, spoke French and wanted their daughter to learn Russian in the little school so that one day she could work in a larger city.

Seated under a fig tree in the school yard, Fanny pouted and squeezed her belly with her hands. It was almost mid-day and she was anxiously waiting for the only meal of the day even if it wasn't to her liking. She worried that they would give her that horrible corn-flour gruel, which the country folk had prepared for years. She could only abide it mixed with cheese and sour cream, a dish the Romanians called *mămăligă cu brânză și smântână*. Her grandmother loved that sour cream, pronounced "shmetene" in

Yiddish, and added it to everything: to cucumbers in brine, to herring (when there was any), to *vareniki* stuffed with cheese and onion, and especially to latkes, Fanny's favorite potato croquettes. But the girl accepted the free lunch from school without a word of protest.

She had just finished her serving when she caught sight of her cousin Simon—a serious and determined twelve-year-old boy who was very grown-up for his age— running in through the entrance. He shouted at her in alarm, which made her get to her feet.

"Come on, Fanny! They've sent me to bring you home right away because I can run faster than your mom."

"But why?"

"Because something dangerous is going on in the village and we must go into hiding. Hurry up, hurry up, they're wait—"

Without stopping to explain to the teacher, Simon dragged her by the arm and forced her to run with him over the dirt roads.

Fanny's mother was already waiting for them outside with a little suitcase full of clothes, black bread and a piece of cheese.

"Fanny, don't be afraid, but we're going to spend a few days at Uncle David's farm. There's no time to waste. Nothing has happened in Yawo yet, but they say that there are a lot of riots in Kishinev, where many Jews live."

Then and there they climbed onto a cart with

other people, and the two horses set off at a trot along the country path toward the forest they could see in the distance. The grown-ups spoke quietly of things she did not understand but found terrifying.

No one bothered them in the countryside. When they were able to return to Yawo, they were told that on the same day in February 1903 that Simon had come to the little school to rescue her, a tragic pogrom had taken place in Kishinev. On that first day of Easter, a crowd led by some priests and the tsar's Cossacks on horseback had attacked people in the streets with sabers and burned more than six hundred houses with no fear of the consequences. The survivors who could left for Palestine or far-off America, where other Jews organized massive financial assistance to help them emigrate.

Fanny grew up in the village but saw less and less of her cousin. It was said Simon had joined the anarchists to protect workers and peasants who fell victim to Russian abuse. In 1905, he took part in the workers' rebellion, which foreshadowed the Russian Revolution, and fought with the crew of the battleship Potemkin. The sailors had mutinied against their officers' brutal and tyrannical regime. The last straw was when the sailors were expected to eat a borsht with worm-infested meat. The rebels killed several of their superiors, took over the ship, and headed toward Odessa. When the army surrounded the port and the ship, the rebels decided to blow up the famous theater, where the leadership assembled. Simon was fighting nearby, on the stairs that went down to the port on the Black Sea, when the sailors attacked. The port was almost destroyed, but both he and the theater survived the attack.

One day in 1908, Simon, who was being hunted down by the Russian authorities, secretly went to say goodbye to Fanny before boarding a freighter and going into exile in Argentina. Neither could imagine that this would be the last time they would ever see each other again.

Buenos Aires, 1913-80

After the great pogrom of Kishinev, as well as other lesser ones, anti-Semitic persecution became more frequent and, for several years, Fanny's life was reduced to doing domestic chores and learning to cook with her grandmother, who considered this essential to getting an educated and hard-working husband. She learned to write at home but did not return to the village school or study Russian, which she never spoke fluently. She never learned anything new about Simon, only rumors that he continued down his political path in Argentina. Eventually the messages stopped altogether. In 1913, when the situation for the Jews of Bessarabia became intolerable, her parents sent her off on her own to join Uncle David, who was already in exile in Buenos Aires, where he worked as a tailor.

When my grandmother Fanny arrived in her new home, which she had pictured as an exotic and remote country, her Uncle David and his children were waiting for her at the port. She was disappointed not to see Simon.

"Uncle David," she asked alarmed, "why didn't Simon come to meet me?"

Her uncle took his time responding, as though wondering sadly how much he could tell her.

"Look, Fanny, your cousin Simon couldn't come because since 1909 he's been held at a prison far away in Ushuaia, in southern Argentina, and we're unable to visit him."

"But why, Uncle? What happened?" she asked, crying bitterly.

"Simon was an anarchist in Russia, and when he arrived here he encountered poverty and saw that the government and police mistreated the workers, just like the Cossacks back there. He soon connected with local anarchists and began organizing strikes and demonstrations downtown. He was finally caught and sentenced to many years in prison."

"But what did he do to get sent so far away?"

"We don't know what happened, Fanny. He was young, only eighteen years old, but even so they sent him to Ushuaia like other dangerous prisoners. We don't think he's guilty, that the charges are false, but we cannot help him. Best not to talk about this with anyone—as Jewish refugees, we have challenges enough and there are anti-Semites here too. Best not to attract attention."

They never spoke of Simon again, either in public or among themselves, for almost forty years. I didn't even know he existed until 1978, when I unexpectedly learned the details of the drama he was central to.

What I remember about Fanny—we called her Lita—was her motherly warmth and her ability to relate to other people thanks to her culinary expertise: she cooked with both love and skill. She was not much of a conversationalist and learned Spanish only to get by. When I was a boy, she taught me some words in Yiddish, the language she spoke with her husband, Lito, and their three daughters. But I could never coax anything out of her when it came to her life before Argentina.

"Lita," I asked one day, "won't you speak to me a little in Russian? Just a few words so I can hear how it sounds."

"I don't like Russian. I don't remember," she said after a long pause, looking at me as though she were suspicious of my thoughtless request.

"But how can you not remember if you were there?" I insisted brazenly.

"Because in Bessarabia ugly things happened. There were pogroms and we were always in hiding."

After that we never touched on the matter again and I had to turn to my father and the encyclopedia to learn what she was talking about. It seemed like a veil she could not take off, as if she had relegated all her past life to her unconscious. But she never forgot the art of cooking. She even perfected it, in particular her mother's specialties. She was generous and open to requests and suggestions. During my medical residency, I used to phone her and invite myself to lunch at her house, which provided a refuge from the tasteless hospital food. One of my favorite dishes was *prakes*, cabbage leaves stuffed with minced meat and spices in a sauce made from tomatoes and onions. To my surprise, other people did not know them by that name, unless they were Jews from a shtetl in southern Romania, because in Ukraine they are called *halupki*, and in Russia they are *golubtsy*, sometimes made with a mixture of beef and pork.

As boys, we would from time to time visit other exiles from the Bessarabia shtetl with my grandparents. In the neighborhood tenement lived an unschooled family with three adult children. Asher, the most advanced intellectually, was a manufacturer of leather goods, billfolds, woman's wallets, and gloves. Motl was a *cuéntenic*, a door-to-door salesman of general provisions and clothes (you could pay in monthly installments, which he recorded by hand in a notebook and scrupulously monitored). And Velvl (or Vélvele), the youngest, had a severe neurological and cognitive disability that was never treated. Vélvele imagined wearing a watch on his right wrist and could tell us the time whenever we cruelly asked him to, to make fun of him.

We overlooked our own flaws and unethical behavior. But we repaid our moral debt when we played alone in the courtyard, where a somewhat demented old man, who often sat under a fig tree, terrorized us. The crazy man knew how to roll back his upper eyelids with a toothpick, revealing the reddish, watery membrane underneath and frightening children when their parents and grandparents were not around.

On Saturday nights, one of my grandmother brothers, who had emigrated from Odessa, would come around with friends to play poker, while 78s cheerfully played klezmer music in the background. During the many brilliant games, the players enjoyed salads made from tomato, herring, onion, and *shmetene*, the ubiquitous sour cream. I loved going to buy it from the incredibly dark tiny shop on Boedo Street, which belonged to a Russian Jew who ladled the cream from huge barrels. I acquired a taste for these delicacies and for the music of Aaron Lebedeff, a traditional Yiddish singer from Bessarabia. But now I realize that in all those years I never heard family or friends mention the existence of Cousin Simon or his imprisonment in a faraway jail.

In 1978, on a flight to Buenos Aires, I read In Patagonia, which Bruce Chatwin had recently published, for the first time. The exciting account of his adventures through the extreme south of Argentina, to Ushuaia and then Punta Arenas in neighboring Chile, reminded me of my student trips in Patagonia. We travelled to regions that were rarely visited, except by other young backpackers, with little money or good equipment for exploring. Our most expensive investments were leather boots and hand-made sleeping bags, with duvet escaping through all the seams. We had little outerwear, almost no waterproof clothing at all, and we were cold a good part of the time. We trekked, with unreliable maps and badly signed trails, to camp by the edge of some blue lake. Our dream was to someday arrive at the mythical city of Ushuaia, a place that was out of our reach because of its remoteness and our lack of resources. Instead, we satisfied ourselves by reaching Esquel, in the province of Chubut, founded by the Welsh in 1895. We had the pleasure of traveling on La Trochita, the tiny narrow-gauge train, known today as the "Old Patagonian Express" because of Paul Theroux's book. One day in Esquel we met an air force major who was interested in chatting with medical students like us. He said that he had an "affinity for doctors" and that his liver was weak (surely due to drinking). In the morning, he had to fly in a military plane to Ushuaia and we begged him to let us accompany him. To our great surprise, he agreed. We arrived, excited, at the airport at four in the morning to meet him. The major turned up at about five surrounded by a large retinue of women and children with numerous suitcases. We learned that, as his family was coming along, the flight was full, which he "greatly regretted." My hopes of visiting the utopian city were put on hold for many years.

In his book, Chatwin described several unusual characters, such as the bank and train robbers Butch Cassidy and Sundance Kid, and other revolutionary and anarchist refugees who added color to the region—including the heroic and risk-taking behavior of one Simon Radovitzky, celebrated prisoner in the penal colony at Ushuaia. In 1908, during a strike and march through the northern neighborhood of Buenos Aires, Radovitzky had blown up the fearsome chief of police, Colonel Falcón.

As soon as I arrived in Argentina, I began to question my mother about the prisoner's name. With great reluctance, and after a long silence, she confirmed that it was Simon, my late grandmother Fanny's forgotten cousin. In this way I fortuitously learned that he existed as well as the terrible reasons for his imprisonment—a prolonged family secret. From that day on, my curiosity about Simon complemented my dream of visiting Ushuaia until it became an obsession, which I would only satisfy many years later, once I was an established professional in the United States.

Ushuaia, 2001 to the present

The plane was chilly, and our light clothes were only suitable for the December summer in Buenos Aires. After the turbulence over Patagonia, we quickly descended toward the goal we had when we were young: legendary Ushuaia in Tierra del Fuego. We landed about 100 meters from the terminal and, because there was no jet bridge, made our way down the airplane steps. We imagined the city would be sunny and warm, but it greeted us with 70 mile-an-hour winds on the runway and an unexpected snowfall that almost completely covered us in white by the time we entered the airport. This icy introduction made us think of the torture Simon would have suffered in his southern prison.

The city is situated at the southernmost end of

the island of Tierra del Fuego, at the edge of South America, and separated from Antarctica by only 600 kilometers of sea. The locals considered it the "end of the world," and a local winery had appropriated the name for its wines. Because it is below the 42nd parallel, it was and still is a duty-free port. Paradoxically, many beneficiaries of this free ride overlook the years of tragedy and suffering when the penal colony still existed.

In the morning, the low, colored houses framed against snowy mountains and facing the brilliant, blue and turbulent ocean reminded us of Juneau, Alaska, in the opposite extreme of North America. While our friends enjoyed a cruise through the Fuegian Channels, my wife, Diana, and I headed to the Museum at the End of the World to research my relative and his misadventures. The building was small, and in the main hall a teacher recounted the city's history for a group of elementary school children, who seemed fascinated by the story. When the talk was over, we introduced ourselves.

"Miss, excuse us for listening in without permission, but we loved your class."

"But of course, tourists are always welcome. We have so much to tell the children: our long history, the Yaghans and the Ona, our indigenous peoples and English heritage, like the Thomas Bridges family and Darwin's voyage in the Beagle. As you know, we border the channel of the same name."

"Actually, although we are tourists, we have a special interest in the history of the penal colony.

A cousin of my grandmother, his name was Simon Radovitzky, was imprisoned there for years. Could we see any documents from that time?"

"You don't say! Your relative was a notorious prisoner, but I'm surprised to see you. I don't recall anyone from your family coming to learn about him. Only historians or anarchists like himself have come through here. Come with me. I can show you photos and documents."

The teacher, who was also the museum's director, showed us into a smaller room that housed the library and archive. The wall was covered with old photos, and she stopped in front of the portrait of a thin man, whose curiously triangular face was smooth except for a very fine moustache under an aquiline nose. He looked undernourished but defiant.

"This was Radovitzky, one of our most celebrated prisoners. He was imprisoned for more than twenty years and then released. I think he went to Spain and ended up fighting in the Civil War."

She looked at us curiously, perhaps searching for some resemblance in me or trying to guess what I was feeling. Then she offered to show us other old photos. It was my first chance to learn about Simon, whom our family had consigned to oblivion. A cold wind blew in through one of the half-opened windows. Suddenly I felt a very long way from home, at the "very edge of Earth," as Lucas Bridges wrote in his book, The Uttermost Part of the Earth. Simon must have thought he was in the antipodes of his native land, Bessarabia, almost another planet. The only similarity he would find was between the brutality of the prison guards and tsar's Cossacks of his youth.

"I can tell you that this man was beloved by the prisoners, who nicknamed him 'the angel of Ushuaia," the teacher said. "They admired him for his inner strength and for resisting the endless torture the prison director subjected him to. They recognized his humanity and his resistance to dictatorship, which mitigated the fact that he assassinated Falcón. Finally, a populist support group in the capital managed to get him released after twenty-one years in prison. Here's a detail that may be of interest to you," she continued. "It's a photo of the MV Monte Cervantes, a ship that was wrecked at Ushuaia in the 1920s. Some prisoners, including Radovitzky, were forced to rescue those who were shipwrecked."

"What a coincidence!" Diana suddenly interjected. "Aida, an old friend of my mother's, was a passenger on the Cervantes and one of the survivors of that shipwreck. Maybe Simon rescued her, just like he helped hide your grandmother, Fanny?"

While my family ignored Simon's existence, there are anarchists today who still try to emulate him. Two years ago, during a visit to Buenos Aires, we stayed in a hotel two hundred meters from La Recoleta, the most famous cemetery in the city, where the remains of aristocratic families and distinguished citizens are laid to rest, Colonel Falcón among them. Curiously, his tomb is also at the same distance from Callao and Quintana, the corner where he was killed.

As we were about to take a quick nap, a heavy explosion outside shook the hotel. When we woke up later, everything was once again calm, and we turned on the TV to watch the news. The first thing the presenter said completely took us aback:

"Breaking news," he said with a trace of a smile. "Two hours ago, at La Recoleta cemetery, a couple of anarchists tried to detonate a bomb in front of Colonel Falcón's tomb on the anniversary of his death. They entered the cemetery when it was just about to close. One of them wore a blond wig and was disguised as a woman in a wheelchair. The other gently pushed her. When they arrived at Falcón's tomb, the one who was dressed as a woman set the bomb, but then decided to take a selfie as a keepsake. The bomb accidentally went off at the same time, amputating his hand and taking away almost half of his face. Police are investigating possible contacts with other anarchist groups."

We sat on the bed, mouths open, facing the unlikely fact that our trip had coincided with modern-day copycats deciding to mimic my relative's behavior a hundred years later.

Neither the press nor the anarchists knew that at the moment of the explosion gone wrong—in an equilateral triangle running from the tomb of Falcón to the corner where the murder took place in 1908, to the hotel—were possibly Simon Radovitsky's only, or last, relatives in Argentina.

Seattle, 2020

A few weeks ago, while browsing the Internet for information about this story, I discovered by chance that in 2016 an Argentine writer had published an illustrated book:

Prisoner 155, subtitled *Simon Radovitzky.*

It was not the first time I had come across key information concerning the subjects of my short stories, but this discovery touched a strong chord in me. I immediately thought of my mother and grandmother, who died without knowing the tragedy that befell our ancestor from Bessarabia.

I wasted no time getting my hands on the book. It was beautifully illustrated by the great cartoonist and narrator, Agustín Comotto, who is now based in Catalonia. The text contained solid historical references from several archives and valuable references from a historian friend of Radovitzky's. A few days later we talked on WhatsApp with Agustín, who was as pleased as I was to know of a direct descendant of his biography's subject. To my surprise, he told me that other relatives who were unknown to me had emigrated to the United States but had changed their surname, perhaps to avoid being linked to our common relative. This was not true of another cousin, Simon's sister, Emilia Radovitzky, who I had never heard mentioned. She was not afraid to acknowledge her direct relationship with him and was clear that she was "proud he had killed a murderer."

The existence of my ancestors in Bessarabi and

the appearance of new interconnected characters continue to affect me, cycling endlessly. From the Hindu perspective, life is eternal, it comes and goes like "waves and bubbles in the current of time," as Dr. Nair, my mentor at Trivandrum, patiently explained to me. Recently, while we were doing some repairs at our Mercer Island home, we got to know an expert carpenter, a quiet man who was about fifty years old. He had emigrated from Eastern Europe and only arrived in the United States seven years previously. I never knew whether he was documented although that is not important. He was the first worker to appear early in the morning and focused on his task within minutes. He had a young assistant, who turned out to be his son-in-law, and they spoke in a language I thought was either Russian or Ukrainian.

As usual, at breakfast, I offered him a quality cappuccino made from beans roasted in Venice in northern Italy. His appreciation was palpable. He seemed surprised by the unexpected gesture and, with a shy smile, drank it slowly and with pleasure, and then immediately returned to his woodworking with even greater focus.

"Very good coffee," he commented admiringly on the first day, nodding his head.

On one of these occasions, I took the opportunity to ask something I already suspected: "Elijah, what country do you come from? Are you from Romania like your boss? I heard him speaking in another language with his assistant. Why do they say da like in Russian?"

I did not expect an elaborate answer because his English was basic.

"No, I come from Bessarabia, which is part of Moldova today. My son-in-law is Ukrainian, and I can speak his language as well as Russian and Romanian."

I was truly amazed to hear once again the name of a region I imagined had disappeared or been merged with neighboring countries.

"Elijah," I replied with some excitement, "my family also came from Bessarabia. My grandmother escaped there to Argentina. She was from Yawo, a very small village. You probably don't know it. My wife's grandparents also come from Kishinev and Akkerman, which were larger cities."

He was so surprised that he stopped working for a few seconds. "Of course I know Chišinau, which was known as Kishinev in Yiddish, and my brother lives in Akkerman, though now we call it Belgorod-Dnestrovskyy!"

His excitement was notable, as was mine when I realized we were alike. From that moment on, he showed even greater dedication and professional pride, and a desire to satisfy his new customer especially. When I asked him to fix the broken legs of one of Diana's desks, the result was spectacular and of high quality: it was better than new. I tried to tip him, but he took a long time to accept, and then he said something strange:

"Tip is not necessary. You're special, like brother. You serve me good coffee in the morning. It's blessing for me, and I want to bless you back. God bless," he added, a phrase he must have learned from the Protestants here.

"Elijah...it's an interesting, deeply religious name. We would say '*Eliahu*' in Hebrew."

"Yes! *Eliahu* is biblical name. A prophet. My last name is M … it could be … I'm not sure."

Again he smiled shyly as if it were a subject he knew well. I thought his surname was decidedly Jewish, although the God bless suggested he was a Christian like his son-in-law. I might speculate that his Jewish family in Bessarabia had to convert to Christianity years back to survive anti-Semitism and the repeated persecutions by the Russians, or the Romanians, or the Ukrainians, and the Germans in World War II.

When the project came to an end on a Friday evening, Elijah came to say goodbye and formally handed me a piece of paper with his name and address, his telephone number, and the well-known phrase, handwritten this time: God bless! We both wore masks to protect us from COVID-19, but I gave him a warm handshake, ignoring the recommendation for social distancing. My brand-new friend, with a big smile and real pride, unexpectedly but clearly said in Hebrew: Shabbat Shalom!

II – ESPAÑOL

TRAVESÍA EN BIRMANIA

Anh Win, un joven delgado con una sonrisa pensativa, sentado en un banco del aeropuerto de Yangón, esperaba la llegada de nuestro avión, que venía atrasado. Como nos contó más tarde, algunos soldados bien armados patrullaban la antigua sala de espera, pero él no les dio excusas para ser interrogado. Como la mayoría, estaba vestido discretamente, con una camisa blanca de algodón, *lungui* tradicional de un azul claro y ojotas de plástico. En lugar de repasar el itinerario para sus clientes aún desconocidos, reflexionaba sobre su flamante liberación de la cárcel de su pueblo.

Nuestro contingente de cuatro amigos de Estados Unidos y Canadá estaba eufórico ante el inminente aterrizaje. Hasta ese momento, el viaje a este país asiático sólo habíamos podido soñarlo. Mucho antes de emprenderlo, nos habíamos preguntado si sería ético visitar una nación bajo dictadura militar, en el que la mayoría de los grandes hoteles y los principales negocios son propiedad del ejército y están bajo su control. Los amigos conocedores de Asia insistían en que la gente trabajadora nos daría la bienvenida, ya que dependía de los extranjeros. Esta opinión prevaleció y, al fin, estábamos llegando al destino largamente imaginado.

Nuestro intento previo de llegar a Birmania había fracasado años antes, cuando un terremoto causó el tremendo tsunami del día de Navidad e inundó las costas de Indonesia, Tailandia y Birmania, matando a más de 200.000 personas en pocos minutos. Poco después, *Burma News,* en Bangkok, la voz de los exiliados de la oposición, había declarado en Internet que los animales fueron los primeros en sentir el terremoto, pues miles de escorpiones venenosos salieron a la superficie en el terreno de la Universidad de Yangón. No necesitábamos más razones para cancelar el viaje.

—Bienvenidos a Myanmar —se presentó el joven que nos esperaba con un cartelito con nuestros nombres—. Soy Anh Win, su guía. Si me permiten, puedo ayudarlos con sus documentos y la aduana. El chófer está afuera con una camioneta para llevarlos al hotel. —El hombre resultó ingenioso y bien preparado. En pocos minutos estábamos cruzando el cansado asfalto de la capital. Viniendo de Bangkok, con sus neones, rascacielos y *skytrain,* el salto a Yangón fue como un paso atrás en el tiempo, a una ciudad colonial que había visto pocos cambios en el siglo pasado. De inmediato nos cautivaron la actividad y los trajes multicolores de la multitud. De pronto, al fondo de una larga avenida inclinada, avistamos por vez primera una estatua colosal, de oro brillante, contra la bruma de la populosa ciudad. Yo hubiese saltado de la furgoneta para explorar el Shwedagon, el principal templo budista, un objetivo primordial de nuestro viaje. Pero me contuve al recordar el consejo de nuestra amiga Mariana de subir al amanecer los incontables escalones de la pagoda, como los peregrinos más devotos.

Llegar a la Residencia del Gobernador fue otro retorno a los tiempos del *Raj,* cuando los británicos gobernaban el subcontinente indio, incluyendo Birmania, hasta la independencia en 1948. Era una mansión romántica de estilo colonial que databa del año 1920. Aceptamos el trago de bienvenida en un jardín brillante de un verde tropical, con estanques jalonados de loto, mientras una brisa suave nos perfumaba. Respirando profundamente, se percibía el aroma de las orquídeas, el jengibre antorcha roja y la *Amherstia nobilis,* conocida aquí como la 'reina de los árboles floridos'.

Siguieron las presentaciones. Nuestros nombres eran difíciles de articular para el guía, que había manejado los arreglos con eficiencia.

—¿Qué significa tu nombre, Anh Win? Nos gusta y tiene un buen ritmo —le pregunté para romper el hielo, ya que estaríamos juntos durante las próximas dos semanas.

—Quiere decir 'brillante e inteligente'; son nombres comunes en Myanmar.

—¿Cómo deberíamos llamar a tu país, Myanmar o Birmania?

—Los británicos le decían Birmania, pero hoy nuestro Gobierno prefiere usar Myanmar. Si no les importa, sería preferible usar el nombre moderno. Pronto les servirán la cena en el jardín. Más tarde, si lo desean, podrían sentarse en el bar Kipling. Yo estaré aquí a las 8, después del desayuno, para llevarlos a la pagoda de Shwedagon, nuestro templo más importante.

En la ficción, los personajes principales deben superar obstáculos. En los años 20, cuando Somerset Maugham visitó por primera vez la entonces llamada Rangún, casi tuvo que irse sin ver el Shwedagon, "porque los birmanos tenían ciertos reglamentos que la religión budista no exigía, y humillar a los occidentales era el objeto de los reglamentos". Obviamente, ya que los birmanos odiaban a los colonizadores británicos. Mi obstáculo, sin embargo, fue subir descalzo por la larga escalera, ya que sufría de una severa fascitis plantar. Pero, una vez en la cima, me maravillé viendo una extensa terraza, salpicada de innumerables santuarios y pagodas, y una multitud de feligreses budistas, desparramados con la confusión de un mercado de pueblo. Algunos hombres y mujeres se deslizaban silenciosamente con los pies descalzos, encendiendo velas o pegando láminas de oro sobre budas de todos los tamaños. Aquí y allá, en posición de *padmasana*, unos monjes, con hábitos de color azafranado, meditaban y, a juzgar por sus pechos inmóviles, parecían no respirar. Este nivel de meditación profunda quizá fuera inalcanzable para nosotros, los occidentales.

La atmósfera de espiritualidad y el respeto que transmite Shwedagon al visitante, con sus imágenes y colorido caleidoscópico, eran inigualables. Pero era tiempo de continuar nuestro itinerario hacia nuevos horizontes. Otra vez en la calle, nos reunimos en una casa de té con Anh Win, quien nos explicó la siguiente etapa: un corto vuelo a Sittwe, en el mar de Andamán, donde abordaríamos una barcaza de río hacia las ruinas de Mrauk U, escondidas en la selva. Su anuncio me recordó las imágenes de Sittwe que había visto en línea: un polvoriento enclave tropical, con murciélagos enormes colgando boca abajo de altos árboles en unas calles de la ciudad. Un video publicado por un viajero alemán mostraba una peluquería surrealista, en donde barberos de piel oscura secaban a mano, con un abanico de papel y bambú, el cabello de los clientes, ya que la mayoría del país carece de electricidad, y los artículos eléctricos no son de fiarse. Descubrir esta barbería era uno de mis objetivos fotográficos...

Llegar a Sittwe fue una regresión a lo que el sudeste asiático debió haber sido antes de las dos guerras mundiales. El escenario de esta ciudad fronteriza era evocador de la cinematografía en blanco y negro de *El arpa birmana*. Recordé a un soldado japonés que se niega a creer que la guerra ha terminado y monjes desolados con cabezas rapadas vagando en el paisaje infinito, inseguros si todavía están vivos o son los fantasmas de antaño.

Nuestro infalible guía aceptó mi pedido de tomar un tuk tuk abierto, lo suficientemente grande para todos, para explorar las calles polvorientas. Yo necesitaba una vista despejada para mi cámara fotográfica, y sentir una conexión directa con el pueblo.

Después de solo unos minutos de girar entusiasmados, nos encontramos con la barbería de mis visiones. Aunque pequeña, era un paraíso para un fotógrafo obsesionado en reflejar "el elemento humano". Los barberos parecían malnutridos y de tez más oscura que Anh Win u otros birmanos, como atormentados por un profundo sufrimiento. Su mirada me hizo pensar en un perro maltratado por su dueño y temeroso de otros humanos. De hecho, estábamos frente a los rohinyás, los descendientes musulmanes de antiguos inmigrantes de Bangladés. Los llamados "bengalíes" eran una minoría rechazada, indocumentada, sin derecho a servicios sociales, agua o atención médica. Había leído en un periódico inglés que, hacía apenas dos semanas, una muchedumbre budista había linchado a un rohinyá —acusado falsamente de violar a una mujer birmana— quizá frente a esta misma peluquería en la calle principal.

Para mejorar mis posibilidades fotográficas, luego de consultar con nuestro guía, se me ocurrió pagarle a un barbero cinco veces el precio de un servicio regular. De ese modo pude sentarme en su silla fingiendo un corte de cabello, con una vista abierta al pequeño salón. Emocionado, oprimí repetidamente el disparador de mi Leica, concentrándome en todos los personajes. Como había visto en el video, después de lavar el cabello de los clientes, lo secaban largamente a mano con un abanico. La elegancia de los movimientos hubiera despertado la envidia de cualquier española paseándose por las ramblas de Barcelona. Un secador eléctrico descansaba inútilmente sobre un mostrador.

Anh Win se relacionaba con los rohinyás con su manera habitual, relajada y acogedora. Más tarde nos explicó que la primera ministra, Aung San Suu Kyi, (a quien llamó respetuosamente "la Dama") deseaba proteger a los rohinyás de los militares, lo que era difícil, ya que ella permanecía bajo detención domiciliaria. Anh Win era reacio a criticar abiertamente al ejército, pero obviamente pertenecía a la oposición silenciosa. Como muchos otros birmanos, veneraba a "la Dama" y tenía grandes esperanzas de un futuro más libre en Birmania. Nunca pensamos que la situación de la minoría rohinyá estaba a punto de cambiar dramáticamente para peor. O que los militares harían un violento golpe de estado unos años después, declarando la ley marcial y matando indiscriminadamente a cientos de manifestantes desarmados.

Sittwe era nuestro punto de partida para llegar a Mrauk U, una ciudad remota y legendaria, redescubierta hace solo un cuarto de siglo. Entonces, la única manera de viajar a Mrauk U era tomar un ferri al amanecer por el río Kaladan para una travesía de seis horas. Según nuestro guía, pocas personas han visitado ese lugar, pues requiere un espíritu bien aventurero. Él había alquilado una barcaza de río que había visto mejores días. El piloto y dos marineros, jóvenes birmanos sonrientes, se mantuvieron a distancia, observando con cuidado el tráfico fluvial. El curso río arriba siguió por un tributario que se hizo más estrecho a medida que avanzábamos. De vez en cuando, viejas pagodas se alzaban imponentes sobre el río. Pronto oscureció y luego, en una noche negra sin estrellas,

las costas quedaron invisibles, excepto por un raro fuego de cocina en los campos. Nos alarmó que no hubiese luces a bordo (con la excepción de una débil lámpara en la letrina), ni luces de navegación, pero a veces podíamos sentir o escuchar otra barcaza yendo en la dirección opuesta, casi rozando la nuestra. O bien estos marineros tenían una visión extraordinaria, o bien navegaban de memoria por las curvas del río. Una vez probé mi poderosa linterna en el lado de babor, pero inmediatamente me gritaron que la apagara, para no perturbar su visión nocturna. Fue un viaje muy pacífico, ya que no podíamos ni leer ni movernos, en un estado similar a la meditación. Finalmente, hubo un poco de conmoción al llegar a un hotel en la selva, donde unos mozos nos esperaban para mostrarnos los bungalós.

El alojamiento no habría sido muy diferente en los viejos tiempos coloniales, cuando los británicos con la Compañía de las Indias Orientales llegaban a las estaciones selváticas aisladas para supervisar la tala o las operaciones mineras, produciendo teca o rubíes para la exportación. A la mañana siguiente, un joven nos aconsejó alejarnos del hermoso estanque que teníamos enfrente y cuidarnos de las serpientes venenosas. Poco después del desayuno, Anh Win trajo una camioneta con un conductor, listo para visitar un polvoriento mercado local. Enseguida nos sorprendieron sus filas de costureras y sastres con máquinas de coser a pedal; un monje muy arrugado estaba comprando un ramo de flores exóticas y, con una expresión imperturbable, pagaba con puñados de dinero local; y había innumerables comerciantes de alimentos, vendiendo productos, exóticos para nosotros. Un hombre estaba sacrificando pollos para vender y ofrecía los restos sangrientos directamente sobre el suelo fangoso. En ese momento decidí nunca más comer pollo en Birmania.

Entrar en Mrauk U, en el estado de Rakhine, destrozado por las guerras, nos exaltaba la imaginación. Man Pa, el rey de Arakán, lo había fundado aproximadamente en 1535. En 1780, este reino independiente se extendía más de 400 millas a lo largo de las llanuras costeras y los pantanos de manglares que bordeaban la bahía de Bengala. En la ciudad amurallada, musulmanes y budistas servían lado a lado en la corte real. Holandeses, portugueses, chinos y otros comerciantes extranjeros vivían en su propio barrio próspero, comerciando con especias, textiles, opio, azufre y pimienta, a cambio de arroz y marfil. Esos días de gloria terminaron en 1784, cuando los invasores birmanos cruzaron la cordillera y conquistaron Mrauk U. La oscuridad cayó sobre la ciudad y sus innumerables templos hasta principios de 1994, cuando la dictadura militar agobiada por la falta de dinero, conocedora de las posibilidades turísticas, con cautela, abrió el área a los extranjeros.

Las ruinas más conocidas de Bagan han sido parcialmente restauradas, pero Mrauk U permaneció intacta. Los templos estaban intercalados con aldeas, en un calmo paisaje rural. A última hora de la tarde, subimos un sendero en decadencia por la jungla hasta la cima de una colina deshabitada. Al caer la tarde, decenas de fuegos de cocina dispersaron un humo azulado sobre la vasta extensión del valle. Estábamos cerca del templo de Shitthaung, con sus 80000 budas, todavía en funcionamiento y rodeado de innumerables pagodas y estupas en la bruma. La exquisita red de templos budistas y defensas militares ha sido propuesta como Patrimonio de la Humanidad por la UNESCO. Trágicamente, después del genocidio rohinyá de 2019, hubo noticias de nuevos combates entre el ejército de liberación de Arakán y el régimen militar birmano. Toda la provincia está de nuevo fuera de los límites para visitantes extranjeros.

Regresando de Sittwe río abajo, el viejo ferri se materializó súbitamente como un barco fantasma frente al nuestro, traqueteando a través de la densa niebla matutina. Mientras lo seguíamos por un rato, giró hacia la derecha en una curva del río medio kilómetro más adelante. En un espejismo causado por la niebla, el ferri parecía deslizarse mágicamente sobre los arrozales, hasta que, de pronto, desapareció. Más tarde, cuando el río se estrechó de nuevo en el corredor de la selva, se me ocurrió que nuestro viaje imitaba al de Fitzcarraldo por el Amazonas, en la película de Werner Herzog. En una escena inolvidable, recorren lentamente la selva virgen, transmitiendo desde un RCA Victor Gramophone arias de Verdi por Caruso, mientras los indios de la orilla escuchan incrédulos, casi hipnotizados. Inspirado por este recuerdo, le pedí a Anh Win que me prestase sus minialtavoces para oír desde el teléfono mi propia música en alto. Mientras la improbable melodía de un tango argentino se dispersaba sobre la jungla birmana, mi esposa y yo nos levantamos espontáneamente para bailarlo en la cubierta de madera podrida, calzados aun con las botas enlodadas.

Volviendo al puerto de partida en la aldea rohinyá, nos encontramos con una escena casi medieval: una extensa fila india de hombres semidesnudos, y unas pocas mujeres llevando sobre sus cabezas pesadas cargas de rocas desde el río, por una larga rampa empinada, hasta la orilla elevada. La mayoría parecían desnutridos e indigentes, descalzos, o unos pocos con sandalias. Este trabajo mal pagado producía piedras pequeñas, pulidas por el río, para usarlas en la construcción de rutas o jardines, hogares o decoración. Pensé en la obligación de recordar que estas rocas venían manchadas por el sudor de los porteadores casi esclavos de este y de otros pueblos.

Mientras nos dirigíamos al hotel, nos cruzamos con un grupo ruidoso de manifestantes en la ruta, fuera de una aldea. Muchos hombres llevaban gorros típicos islámicos. Impresionado por el espectáculo, le pedí a nuestro conductor que se detuviera y me dejara fotografiar al grupo. Anh Min, muy alarmado, le ordenó inmediatamente que nos sacara de allí. A pocos pasos de la aldea, tuvimos que mostrar nuestros documentos en un control militar. Nos dejaron ir, siendo los únicos turistas en esta zona. Pero noté largas gotas de sudor en el delgado cuello de Anh Min, la primera vez que él había transpirado, incluso en un día muy caluroso.

Una vez a salvo en el salón del hotel, invité a

nuestro angustiado guía a acompañarnos con un té. Quería entender su reacción durante el bloqueo. Creíamos que ya para este momento pudiera fiarse de nuestra discreción.

—Todavía estoy inquieto —confesó—. Poco antes de conocerlos me metieron preso, pero me dejaron salir justo para la llegada de su grupo. Pensaba en eso mientras los esperaba en Yangón, sin poder concentrarme en los detalles del itinerario. Fue penoso para todos, especialmente para mi madre.

—¿Por qué te arrestaron, Anh Win? ¿Por causas políticas?

—No, un policía corrupto en mi pueblo me detuvo en la carretera cuando llevaba a un turista en la motocicleta. Este era un cliente que yo conocía bien, quien me había llamado desde el aeropuerto pidiendo que lo trasladara para explorar las ruinas. No me pude negar.

—No comprendo por qué te metieron en la cárcel, siendo un guía acreditado y bien conocido en tu pueblo.

—Porque hay un reglamento de seguridad que nos prohíbe conducir con un extranjero en el asiento trasero de una motocicleta. Nadie lo respeta, pero el policía insistió en embolsarse una multa, y yo me negué. El turista no pudo ayudar y tuvo que andar el resto del camino con su mochila. Me las arreglé para darle el número de teléfono de mi madre para hacérselo saber.

—¿Cuánto tiempo te tuvieron preso? ¿Cómo saliste?

—Estuve una semana en la cárcel. El primer día fue terrible porque solo me dieron un poco de arroz rancio para comer, y el agua estaba sucia. Tenía miedo de enfermar, porque no podía comer y beber con confianza. Otros presos no se sentían bien y no había atención médica.

—¿Cómo pudo ayudar tu madre?

—Nuestra familia ha vivido aquí por muchas generaciones y tenemos una fábrica de muebles conocida, en la que usamos teca y otras maderas exóticas, para exportar a China. Pero, en los viejos tiempos, mi abuelo se ocupaba de la minería de piedras preciosas, y había ocultado unos rubíes de diferentes tamaños. Mi madre recuperó dos de las piedras más bonitas y fue a ver al jefe de policía de nuestro pueblo, a quien conocía. Aunque era abusador, ella pudo apaciguarlo con un soborno. Más tarde, la dejaron traerme algo de comida casera y unas botellas de agua potable. No me golpearon, pero la policía y otros presos me acosaban bastante, hasta que me trasladaron a una celda más pequeña para mí solo, y entonces me sentí más seguro. Finalmente, me dejaron ir, pero aún estoy inquieto cerca de la policía. Ellos saben que somos opositores y que mi familia apoya a la Dama. Debemos tener cuidado, por favor, que esto quede entre nosotros.

Nuestro guía, ya casi un amigo, apreció tener un hombro en que apoyarse. Luego nos invitó a conocer a su familia y a visitar la fábrica. Su madre era una mujer elegante, de mediana edad, de gran aplomo y determinación. Claramente, tenía herramientas para neutralizar a un jefe de policía corrupto. En el taller, la calidad y la artesanía eran asombrosas, considerando que todo estaba hecho a mano, sin energía eléctrica. El capataz, que hablaba bien inglés, explicó que la corriente era intermitente, y las piezas de repuesto eran difíciles de conseguir. Por eso prefieren depender de sus propias manos. Están orgullosos de su trabajo y temen que el uso de equipos eléctricos les haga perder las habilidades transmitidas por generaciones, una actitud habitual en todo el país. La artesanía era igualmente superlativa, entre carpinteros, constructores de barcos, fabricantes de cigarros y especialmente los joyeros, capaces de crear exquisitas filigranas con metales preciosos.

Nuestro interés (sobre todo el mío) en el ritual y la filosofía budistas, así como en la meditación, habían impresionado a Anh Win. Una mañana, después de unas llamadas telefónicas, tuvo una idea sorprendente:

—Mi maestro budista, el abad del monasterio de Mahāgandāyon, en Mandalay, acaba de responder que está dispuesto a vernos en privado. Habla bien inglés. ¿Qué les parece incluir esto en el itinerario?

Encantados por la oportunidad única, fuimos a visitar el monasterio, situado en un paraíso tropical y verdoso en Amarapura. De hecho, llegamos antes de las 11 de la mañana, hora del almuerzo para los monjes novicios (y monjas, al otro lado de la calle). Hacen fila, callados y ordenados, para su única comida del día. Luego de observar el almuerzo, dimos un tranquilo paseo por el monasterio, rodeado a veces por animados grupos de novicios. Anh Win nos había indicado que nos dirigiéramos a su mentor como "Hashin" (que curiosamente nos sonaba como "Ha Shem", literalmente "el Nombre" en hebreo, para referirse a Dios en el judaísmo).

Hashin era un hombre sonriente de unos 40 años, delgado y musculoso, recién vuelto de retiro de meditación en la selva del estado de Shan. Su mirada profunda y disposición alerta sugerían que pronto había evaluado nuestra actitud y estaba listo para responder preguntas. Nos sentamos en un duro suelo de hormigón, con las piernas cruzadas, respetando la regla de nunca apuntar con nuestros pies al maestro, una falta de respeto. Dada mi edad, la rigidez de mis articulaciones y la artritis dolorosa, rápidamente me di cuenta de que ya no era material para una estancia prolongada en el monasterio. Igualmente hice todo lo posible por ignorar la incomodidad y prestar atención. Hashin comenzó ansioso por responder preguntas, pero pronto su discurso se convirtió en un monólogo:

—Yo he enseñado *vipasāna*, o meditación de la atención plena, a muchos estudiantes extranjeros que se quedan con nosotros durante diez días, pero en solo una hora, apenas puedo hablarles de los conocimientos básicos. Esta práctica purifica y calma la mente. Al llegar a la vejez, los budistas deben conocerse y tener confianza en sí mismos, para afrontar la muerte.

—Los estudiantes aprenden a sentarse y usar la meditación respiratoria durante al menos media hora, para observar sus sensaciones, sin tratar de controlar su respiración o sus pensamientos. Deben observarlo todo como es, pero no cambiarlo deliberadamente. Después de media hora, en general continuamos con la meditación a pie, y tanto la práctica sentada como caminando se deben hacer en silencio. Pueden observar, pero no modificar ningún pensamiento que los distraiga. Se trata de descubrir la naturaleza efímera de la mente y la materia, hasta lograr la contemplación del Dharma. Para mí, la meditación significa observarse profundamente hasta llegar a la verdadera sabiduría.

Después del corto pero intenso encuentro, compramos varios libros de Hashin sobre el budismo y la democracia, los acontecimientos actuales e incluso la filosofía de la vida matrimonial. Si hubiera sabido que pocas semanas después de nuestra visita algunos monjes budistas y los militares comenzarían el exterminio de una gran parte de la población rohinyá, me hubiese gustado pedirle su opinión sobre estos temas: ¿Cómo justificaba que el pueblo de Buthidaung y el templo, que habíamos visitado y fotografiado, fueran bombardeados por un avión de guerra birmano en 2019? ¿Qué tendría que decir sobre la Dama, quien recibiría el Premio Nobel por su oposición a la junta? Incomprensiblemente, la misma negó más tarde frente a las Naciones Unidas que hubiese persecuciones y se puso del lado de los militares. A pesar de su apoyo a las Fuerzas Armadas, Aung San Suu Kyi fue arrestada en 2021 durante el golpe y, en este momento, se desconoce su paradero.

Alcanzar nuestro destino en el lago Inle fue un ejemplo del carácter tenaz e ingenioso de Anh Win.

Aunque hay caminos de tierra con enormes baches, lo ideal es llegar al hotel en barco desde Nyaungshwe, el pueblo de acceso al lago. Estas lanchas largas, con una sola fila central de tres a cuatro asientos, por lo general pertenecen a los militares, que tienen el monopolio de la mayoría de las empresas. En los últimos años, unos pocos civiles atrevidos habían creado empresas turísticas más pequeñas para competir con los grupos establecidos. Así, Anh Win había invertido en un nuevo barco; con los beneficios iniciales, se había expandido hasta ser dueño de ocho lanchas en el lago Inle. Tuvo el valor de enfrentarse a las autoridades y fue capaz de conducirnos al hotel en una nueva embarcación de su pequeña flota. Llegamos a salvo, aunque en secreto temíamos ser víctimas de un abordaje, ya que los militares no respetan, ni son diplomáticos con los turistas.

Una mañana, Anh Win nos llevó a una pequeña isla de unos cien metros de diámetro, en medio del lago, para una ceremonia en la pagoda Hpaung Daw U. La pequeña playa estaba literalmente invadida por un gran número de embarcaciones similares, que traían a los familiares de los novicios a punto de ser ordenados en el histórico templo budista. Aunque nos rodeaba la multitud de familiares de todas las edades, nos arreglamos para ver la brillante ceremonia desde la puerta principal. La escena era única y exótica, ya que la devoción de los participantes y el significado del momento eran conmovedores. De pronto, mi situación tomó un giro inesperado, porque necesitaba aliviar mi vejiga, y corrí con urgencia en busca de los baños.

En el pasillo principal, los dos baños separados para hombres y mujeres tenían una larga fila de personas con la misma intención. Miré a mi alrededor fuera de la pagoda, pero no había un solo árbol detrás del cual esconderse, y una muchedumbre circulaba por el sendero. Mi única opción era ponerme en fila para esperar turno en los recintos sagrados, siempre descalzo como requieren en un templo. Para mi consternación, el desagüe de ambos inodoros estaba tapado, y la pequeña habitación rebosaba de orina acre y oscura, que llegaba a varios centímetros sobre el suelo. Dado el tamaño de mi próstata y la urgencia de la situación, tuve que hacer de tripas corazón y sumergirme como los otros aldeanos, que parecían mucho menos sorprendidos o angustiados por la inundación. De regreso al hotel, me tomé mucho tiempo bajo la ducha y un jabón entero para depurarme de la consagrada orina birmana.

Este viaje transformador abrió mis ojos y mi corazón a la humanidad de este pueblo con tanta espiritualidad, gracia y talento. El éxito de nuestra travesía lo debemos en gran parte a nuestro guía, el emprendedor navegante del lago Inle. Más aún, agradezco a los barberos que me permitieron grabar un momento de su vida cotidiana con mi cámara y acercarme a la población rohinyá. Pero mucha agua ha corrido bajo el puente desde nuestro viaje, y se han producido cambios profundos en el país. Este grupo étnico ha sido casi exterminado y los sobrevivientes fueron expulsados al campamento de refugiados más grande del mundo, ubicado en Bangladés. En las últimas semanas, la situación de Birmania se ha vuelto más compleja. Las noticias de la BBC muestran imágenes de una sangrienta represión militar de toda la población en las calles de Yangón, Mandalay y otras ciudades. Estas tragedias se suman a una pandemia descontrolada, para la que este régimen no está preparado. Confiamos en que estas catástrofes lleguen pronto a su fin y en que los líderes responsables sean llevados ante la justicia. Mi esposa y yo soñamos con poder subir nuevamente, descalzos y sin dolor, los innumerables escalones del Shwedagon.

MILANESAS

Caminando por un barrio poco habitual, cerca de la Cancillería, en plaza San Martín, unos retorcijones me recordaron que ya era pasado el mediodía y hora de buscar en dónde almorzar. Como es frecuente en Buenos Aires, había un café en la esquina, con el menú del día escrito a mano sobre un cartel en la ventana. Entré sin consultarlo, atraído por el aspecto ordenado y limpio, y porque aún tenía mesas disponibles. Era un viaje relámpago para visitar a mi madre hospitalizada con insuficiencia cardíaca. Esta vez ella no estaba en condiciones de prepararme una de sus inolvidables recetas.

Me senté frente a una ventana y pronto se presentó el mozo a ver qué me gustaría comer.

—¿Qué le ofrezco, caballero? —me preguntó, con amabilidad.

—¿Qué me sugiere, mozo? No soy del barrio y no conozco su especialidad.

—Mire, tenemos solo dos cosas, pero hoy le recomiendo las milanesas con papas fritas. A este muchacho en la cocina le salen como si hubiera aprendido desde que nació. ¿Le gustarían simples o *a caballo?*

—No, simples y con bastante limón. —Su pregunta me hizo sonreír, ya que agregarles un huevo frito encima, y llamarlas *a caballo,* era una costumbre muy argentina.

Mientras esperaba la orden, viendo pasar gente, me quedé pensando en el gusto tan recordado de las milanesas, y en aquel día remoto durante mi residencia en Medicina, en que me había autoinvitado a casa de mi abuela para almorzar este mismo menú. Se daba la situación casi surrealista de que cerraban el hospital debido a una huelga de empleados universitarios. También pensé en la aptitud de los mozos argentinos, que rara vez necesitan escribir una orden, aun las complejas para una mesa de mucha gente, y sin olvidar lo que cada uno deseaba. Las costumbres locales, aprendidas desde mi infancia, eran muy distintas a las que me había habituado luego de tantos años en los Estados Unidos. Reencontrar estas prácticas me hizo sentir otra vez como en casa, habiendo nacido y crecido aquí, aunque de a ratos tuviera una sensación extraña de *depaysement,* un exotismo y desorientación por el cambio de ambiente, como cualquier turista extranjero.

En eso llegó la orden, una suculenta milanesa dorada, acompañada por unas brillantes papas fritas, crocantes y nada grasientas, rodeada por algunas tajadas de amarillo limón. Esta paleta colorida impulsó mi imaginación descontrolada a transformarla en una pintura rústica, digna de un Matisse o de las texturas propias de un Van Gogh. Me quedé saboreando este manjar por un buen rato, hasta que volviera el mozo a ofrecerme el consabido cafecito para completar el almuerzo.

Luego de esta opípara comida, caminé largo y tendido por las calles de la ciudad, rememorando antiguos paseos y coincidencias felices, o a veces trágicas, en las que, misteriosamente, volvían a aparecer otras milanesas. Con el paso de los años, mi madre multiplicaba ya sus estadías en las salas de hospital e incluso de terapia intensiva. Durante una de esas ocasiones en que la visitábamos, mi esposa y yo aprovechamos el tiempo libre en Buenos Aires para pedirle a Rubén, un querido maestro de tango *milonguero,* que nos diera una clase particular.

Quedamos en vernos en la esquina de Entre Ríos y San Juan, un barrio popular que conocí bien cuando joven, muy cerca de mi antiguo colegio secundario. Todo parecía diferente, decrépito como en una película de postguerra, tanto los edificios como el aspecto de algunos vecinos.

Llegamos temprano y recorriendo el barrio nos maravilló en una esquina un gran mural de colores del *Café del Biógrafo,* como antes llamaban al cine, ilustrando una cámara filmadora antigua. Un cartel escrito a mano sobre un papel en la ventana nos atrajo, a mí por lo menos, con un magnetismo casi planetario: "Plato del día: Milanesas a la Napolitana". Ya adentro vimos a algunas señoras con niños corriendo entre las mesas y a un parroquiano bastante entrado en años, dormido sobre un diario, propiedad del establecimiento. Sobre la mesa había una tacita de café expreso vacía, probablemente el mínimo gasto que le permitía quedarse allí por largas horas. El precio de la comida era bajísimo para un turista, de modo que pedimos dos órdenes de milanesas, que nos parecieron gigantes. Llegaron cubiertas por capas sucesivas de *mozzarella,* jamón cocido y una sabrosísima salsa de tomate, que los locales llaman 'tuco'. Este banquete que apenas probamos podría haber alimentado a una familia entera de refugiados famélicos, recién bajados de un barco en el cercano puerto. Hubiera sido insensato descartarlas y se nos ocurrió llevarlas para la cena en el hotel. Esa costumbre, tan común en los Estados Unidos, suscitó de inmediato un encuentro insólito con el mozo.

—¿De veras quiere llevarse lo que queda? Acá la gente no hace eso. A veces las quieren terminar los muchachos de la cocina o las tiramos a la basura. Además, no tengo ningún recipiente para ponerlas, nadie lo pide.

—¡No se ofenda! Sus milanesas son buenísimas, pero desayunamos muy tarde y ahora no tenemos fuerza para terminarlas. Sería un crimen abandonarlas y nos gustaría llevarlas para la casa. Mire, no nos molestaría si las pone dentro de los cartones que usa para la pizza, veo que tiene muchos.

Aceptó a regañadientes y, por supuesto, dejamos una propina sustancial. Entonces salimos caminando hacia la clase, muy orgullosos con los valiosos restos culinarios en el paquetito.

Encontramos a Rubén en la esquina principal y nos dirigimos hacia el departamento de Melinda, su colega y compañera para esta clase. Vivía en una casa de varios pisos, bien pintada, pero con la entrada curiosamente rodeada por una gran jaula de hierro forjado, con dos puertas sucesivas cerradas con llave, como una celda de policía en un pueblito de Wyoming. Alrededor de la jaula había unos cuantos personajes tirados en el piso, dormidos o quizá drogones en coma por sobredosis, lo que explicaba las medidas extremas de los vecinos para protegerse de los indeseables. Al entrar en el departamento casi vacío, excepto por algunos espejos útiles para los bailarines, depositamos sobre una mesa la caja de cartón, sin pensar más en ella. La escena de la entrada había sido muy desagradable, pero logramos olvidarla cuando Rubén nos dio una buenísima clase de tango.

Mientras practicábamos algunos pasos nuevos y corregíamos errores, me distraía el ambiente diferente, trayéndome recuerdos de mi adolescencia en un apartamento similar en el barrio de Barracas. Igual que entonces, por sus ventanas abiertas hacia un patio interior, subían rumores de conversaciones entre vecinos y flotaba un intenso aroma de buena comida desde los pisos inferiores, que imaginamos preparaba alguna vecina, excelente cocinera de barrio. Cuando la clase casi terminaba, notamos de pronto que el cielo se había vuelto plomizo y que la luz disminuía con rapidez. Sin aviso previo, se descargó una tremenda tormenta con truenos y relámpagos, lloviendo a cántaros, como a veces ocurre brutalmente en la capital o en la provincia de Buenos Aires. Al asomarnos por la ventana, vimos que ya la calle estaba inundada y que casi no pasaban vehículos. Rubén y su compañera se alarmaron por nosotros, y sugirieron terminar ya la lección, les pagamos con urgencia y nos lanzamos hacia la salida. Rubén nos abrió apurado las cerraduras sucesivas de la jaula para poder salir. Los drogones seguían dormidos, sin responder a la inundación. Milagrosamente, un taxi se detuvo frente a la entrada y, al bajar una persona corriendo, sin pedir permiso nos precipitamos por la puerta trasera, pidiendo que nos llevara. El conductor se dirigió hacia el hotel, con el auto casi flotando, por la Avenida Entre Ríos. Mientras nos felicitábamos por nuestra buena suerte, al pasar frente al Congreso descubrimos de pronto y con gran tristeza que nos habíamos dejado el cartón con los restos del almuerzo, y que sería imposible volver a recuperarlo en medio de esa tormenta tropical. En ese mismo instante de iluminación nos dimos cuenta de que los aromas que con tanto placer nos distraían durante la clase habían sido los efluvios que emanaba sobre la mesa nuestra olvidada caja con las "milanesas a la napolitana". Más triste aún, por la mañana me llamó Rubén para agradecerme por el exquisito almuerzo que les había dejado "como regalo", y que descubrieron durante la tormenta.

Al día siguiente, luego de visitar a mi madre en el hospital, un impulso me llevó a llamar por teléfono a los pocos amigos que aún me quedaban en Buenos Aires, entre ellos a Victoria, antigua compañera desde los años de la facultad. Nacida en la Patagonia, había crecido en la finca de su familia cerca del Bolsón, en Río Negro. Como muchos otros jóvenes, luego de estudiar abogacía en la Universidad de Buenos Aires, había adoptado la vida en la capital y solo regresaba a la Patagonia en verano y para las fiestas de fin de año con su familia. Sus hermanos se ocupaban de la estancia y de criar los miles de ovejas desparramadas por su extensa propiedad. Para entonces, Victoria había ya publicado varios libros de poesía, ganado premios de la Universidad Católica y tenía poemas publicados en el reconocido *Diario de Poesía*. Nos unían los viajes de mochileros juntos por el sur en tiempos de estudiantes, la admiración por la Patagonia y especialmente por la literatura, si bien yo me interesaba por la prosa y la ficción, y ella, por la poesía. Me recibió esa misma tarde con un vasito de vino para ponernos al día sobre nuestras trayectorias y eventos importantes.

—Como sabrás, hace dos años que estoy divorciada de Alberto, quien decidió dedicarse por completo a la ganadería, como muchos otros de nuestra generación, en el campo. Yo amo la vida ciudadana y las oportunidades intelectuales de esta gran ciudad —me explicó con franqueza. Por supuesto, pensé, ella podía dedicarse de lleno a la poesía gracias a su independencia económica y a la voluntad de sus hermanos de manejar la hacienda en el sur.

—Me sorprende que no prefieras pasar más tiempo en el Bolsón, una zona tan bella, con sus atractivos naturales y culturales. ¿No es un pueblo interesante y progresista?

—Es verdad que les gusta mucho a los turistas, con su mercado de artesanías regionales, los artículos de lana y de cuero, los cuchillos criollos y otras cosas. Pero para nosotros, lo más importante es habernos declarado una "zona libre de la energía nuclear", sin ninguna polución radioactiva. En eso somos únicos en el país. En cambio, nos preocupa una posible erupción del Chaitén, un volcán del lado chileno de la cordillera, que debido a los vientos andinos nos riega sus cenizas con frecuencia y a veces han tenido que evacuar a los habitantes de algunos pueblos cercanos. Como vos sabés, en Chile está la cadena de volcanes más grande y de mayor actividad en el mundo después de la de Indonesia. Esto me tiene sumamente alarmada por mi gente en la Patagonia.

—Supongo que tendrás una nueva pareja —le pregunté con poca diplomacia, para cambiar de tema. No creía que lo del volcán fuese algo tan serio, pero su ansiedad era comprensible. Victoria era muy sensible, como otros poetas, y tenía tendencia a dramatizar.

—Realmente, no tengo a nadie permanente. Salgo a veces con Facundo, un jugador de polo profesional, quien viaja mucho por el mundo para competir, es capitán del equipo y un tipo muy popular, que no tiene la más mínima intención de sentirse prisionero de una divorciada. Mirá, no quisiera interrumpir esta charla, pero esta noche hay reunión de la Sociedad de Poesía de Buenos Aires, una linda organización. Se reúnen en una librería de Palermo. ¿No te gustaría acompañarme? Puede haber lecturas interesantes y podrías conocer a alguna gente de valor. Solo que no tendríamos tiempo para cenar antes de la reunión, ¿qué te parece?

—Me fascina la idea, siempre y cuando yo no tenga que participar en ninguna discusión, sabés que de poesía conozco tanto como de física cuántica.

El sitio era una librería muy bien surtida en literatura en español, sobre todo de América Latina, y pensé volver otro día a elegir algunos volúmenes para llevarme a casa. Unas cien personas de distintas edades, algunos en parejas, en especial jóvenes con expresión intensa e inteligente, vestidos con sencillez, de preferencia con largas melenas, se repartieron en un semicírculo desordenado de sillas. Algunos ya no tan jóvenes y algo más profesorales, se sentaban adelante, cerca del centro, en donde había una mesita con buena luz para leer y presentar sus trabajos. Un señor en particular, con aspecto muy serio y descuidados cabellos grises, quedó algo separado del resto, como si temieran aproximarse a él, o si le hicieran espacio por respeto.

El programa era de lecturas cortas de un poema y, a continuación, unos minutos para preguntas al autor o comentarios breves. Al no conocerlos, me resultaba difícil recordar sus nombres. En general, las preguntas eran técnicas y benévolas, como en familia, aunque en ciertos casos fueron más cortantes y agresivas. En esos tiempos no existían teléfonos celulares para grabar subrepticiamente las presentaciones y tuve que recurrir al lápiz y escribir con rapidez. Un señor regordete ya entrado en años que creo llamaron Padeletti, con la expresión beatífica de un monje budista presentó su poema "Apuntamientos en el ashram", que me impactó por su exotismo y su profundidad. Alcancé a anotar un fragmento:

Si todo es de otro modo,
entonces todo es nada y todo es todo:
en el grano el granado, la granada,
rubí, colmena, sangre y estocada.
La piedra que buscaba el alquimista
está, con cualquier nombre, ante la vista;
no el secreto, la forma solamente…

Un poco más tarde recitó una joven morena y bajita, de grandes ojos negros quien, igual que Victoria, había crecido en la Patagonia. Leyó, como electrizada, su poema "Protecciones", del que anoté unas pocas líneas:

Protección, y todos los libros que amé
Un crucifijo para espantar calaveras
Un sendero de hojas amarillas
Para dar una vuelta en bicicleta por el otoño.

Y luego, impresiones de una infancia placentera en la casa de campo:

Alcohol añejado
Dulce de ciruelas en la cocina
Y un lugarcito cerca de la chimenea
Para apretar los hilos del silencio
A la hora de los cuentos de aparecidos.

Terminadas las lecturas, ya casi las once de la noche, muchos se retiraron, y una minoría se dispersó por la librería. Victoria se unió a un pequeño grupo más selecto y me invitó a acompañarlos para seguir la discusión y socializar en un café del barrio. Acepté, agradecido de que me hubiesen incluido. Más aún, cuando mi amiga me presentó ya en el café, me recibieron amables con algo de curiosidad y con un beso, algo común al conocerse en la Argentina, no solo entre poetas. Esta no era una costumbre entre hombres en mi juventud antes de alejarme del país, lo que distaba de la modalidad anglosajona, y me hizo sentir a gusto rápidamente.

Pronto vino el mozo a tomar nuestras órdenes, que resultaron muy sencillas: un cafecito para todo el mundo. Solo que yo no había comido nada desde el mediodía y se me ocurrió pedirle algo muy común en los cafés de Buenos Aires: un sándwich de milanesa. Eso produjo un movimiento general, la mesa entera se dio vuelta para mirarme con algo de consternación y de sorpresa. Pero mi reacción fue muy rápida también:

—Les pido disculpas, yo soy un invitado de Victoria, vengo de afuera y no conozco bien las costumbres de la Sociedad de Poesía. ¿No me permitirían convidarlos y acompañarme con algo para comer?

Al principio la respuesta del grupo fue tentativa, algunas manos se iban levantando como una ola progresiva, pero en pocos segundos la mesa entera estuvo de acuerdo en pedir ¡lo mismo para todos! Era evidente que la situación económica en la Argentina actual no permitía a los jóvenes poetas y a sus admirados mentores asumir otros gastos que un simple cafecito.

Si bien era yo quien quería conocerlos mejor y comprender sus intereses y personalidades, tuve que responder al agradecimiento y curiosidad de muchos, sorprendidos por la invitación inesperada. Varios imaginaron que yo también era poeta y me defendí como pude, explicando que solo escribía cuentos cortos, pero que no era competente en poesía. El señor respetable de cabellos grises frente a mí en la mesa parecía casi dormido, cabizbajo mirando al suelo, y sin participar en la conversación. La mujer que había leído su poema sobre su juventud en Patagonia fue una de las personas que me interrogó primero:

—¿Viajaste por la Patagonia alguna vez? Quizá hayas reconocido ciertos lugares en mis versos.

—Así es, recuerdo haber pasado por el Bolsón cuando era estudiante y mochilero. Me hubiese gustado volver algún día y quedarme por más tiempo. En tu poema me impresionaron las imágenes sobre escenas domésticas en tu infancia, como las referencias al "dulce de ciruelas en la cocina; un lugarcito cerca de la chimenea ... a la hora de los cuentos de aparecidos". Esta última es una visión muy fuerte de algo que puedo imaginar, pero en la que nunca me tocó participar. En tu casa, ¿quién contaba estos cuentos para asustar a los niños?

—¡Qué bárbaro para recordar algo que dije tan rápidamente...! Mi padre lo invitaba al capataz de la estancia porque era payador y un buen cuentista.

Dándole una copita de aguardiente de caña, lo hacíamos hablar toda la noche.

A todo esto, se fue despertando el señor de cabellos grises y me preguntó sorpresivamente:

—¿Nos vas a decir cuáles son los temas preferidos para tus cuentos?

Antes de que yo pudiese responder, Victoria se me adelantó:

—Les tengo que relatar algo, ya que Armando no conoce los pormenores sobre el destino de su cuento "La muerte paralela de don Quijote". Se refiere a un dramático encuentro de dos médicos legistas, viejos amigos, en un restaurante frente al lago Washington. Lo escribió en inglés y me pidió que lo traduzca al español. Cuando lo hice, me gustó mucho por lo imaginativo, con influencias surrealistas. Sin su permiso, me atreví a enviarlo a concurso en la Sociedad Argentina de Ciencia Ficción. Y no se imaginan: ¡salió premiado! Como él estaba en los Estados Unidos, tuvo que ir su madre muy honrada a recibir el premio, pero sin saber de qué se trataba, y sin poder decir una palabra cuando le preguntaron en público su opinión sobre el cuento. Para colmo esa fue la última sesión de la sociedad, ya que la disolvieron ese año. *"Sic transit gloria mundi!"*

El señor serio y profesoral parecía paulatinamente más alerta y participaba más en la conversación. Dirigiéndose a mí, me sugirió un tema:

—Deberías escribir sobre la gente en esta reunión de hoy. No sería raro que te diéramos material dramático para un cuento corto. Pero entre tanto, como corolario de tu invitación de antes, ¿podrías explicarnos, si lo sabes, el significado de nuestra expresión "la verdad de la milanesa"?

—No sabía que esa frase se usara todavía, porque el lenguaje ha evolucionado. Gracias por recordarme este sabio dicho popular tan argentino. Lo interpreto como una metáfora sobre el significado de la vida en general. Solo que lamento desilusionarlos con una respuesta insuficiente. Prefiero citar lo que nos dijo hoy Padeletti: "Todo es nada y todo es todo", cuando también sugirió que "La piedra que buscaba el alquimista está, con cualquier nombre, ante la vista". Ustedes me han inspirado a escribir sobre este viaje y esta noche. Y confío encontrar un día respuesta a tu pregunta, que resume todo.

Estimulada en parte por el café y por las milanesas, que cortaron el hielo y dieron energía al grupo, la charla continuó por un buen rato. En mi caso, me ayudaron a conectarme con los presentes y a sentirme cómodo entre esta gente. Gracias al contacto humano estaba reviviendo experiencias de mi juventud porteña, las que sumadas a los años de vida en el exterior iban a contribuir a mi desarrollo emocional.

Como era inevitable, terminó la velada y la gente comenzó a levantarse de la mesa. El señor de cabellos grises, cuyo nombre aun no conocía, se acercó para despedirse y para mi gran sorpresa me dio un fuerte abrazo, un beso en la mejilla izquierda, y dijo simplemente: "Suerte con todo, seguí escribiendo", y se retiró sin saludar a nadie más. Un rumor inesperado se esparció entre los que quedaban, estupefactos, en la sala. Victoria se apresuró a decirme, incrédula:

—¿Te das cuenta de que Diego, el decano de la poesía argentina, te dio un beso al despedirse, algo que casi nunca hace, solamente a vos, al único que no conocía en esta reunión? Es inconcebible y a lo mejor un insulto para todos nosotros. Parecía muy depre, aunque eso no es nada nuevo. Por alguna razón lo impresionaste mucho.

Al despedirnos de Victoria en la puerta de su casa, le agradecí por haberme hecho conocer a esta gente fascinante e ilustrada y, algo triste por la separación, ya nostálgico de haber vivido un momento muy especial, seguí camino hacia el hotel cercano. Me quedaban solo dos días para volver a casa, confiando en que mi madre mejorase y le dieran de alta en el hospital.

Mientras esperaba un taxi en la entrada el día de la partida, llegó corriendo el joven de la recepción para avisarme de que tenía una llamada telefónica. Era Victoria, muy alarmada y con voz quebradiza, con un mensaje desconcertante:

—Armando, lo siento por traerte malas noticias antes de tu partida. Acabo de enterarme de que la mañana siguiente a la reunión, la secretaria encontró a Diego muerto frente a su escritorio. ¡Se había pegado un tiro! Esto representa una gran tragedia para nuestra poesía. No tenía otra familia, y probablemente fuimos los últimos en hablar con él, antes de su suicidio. Por si esto fuese poco, te cuento que yo también estoy saliendo de Buenos Aires, porque el volcán Chaitén ha aumentado sumamente su actividad y mi gente me necesita. Es un drama encima de otro.

Pocos días después de mi llegada a Seattle leí en el *New York Times* que habían cancelado todos los vuelos sobre la Patagonia debido a la erupción del volcán Chaitén en Chile. La ceniza volcánica, esparcida por los vientos australes, había afectado especialmente a la región del Bolsón en Argentina. Las grandes fincas estaban cubiertas por una capa tóxica con graves efectos respiratorios y digestivos en los animales, y había matado ya a miles de ovejas, al no poder encontrar agua limpia y vegetación para comer.

Temí entonces que esto tuviera un terrible efecto a largo plazo sobre Victoria, su persona y su propiedad. A partir de ese día perdimos el contacto y no hubo más respuesta a mi correspondencia. Siento que esta tragedia está conectada, aunque en forma incomprensible, con la muerte de Diego, a quien nunca podré explicarle, aún si yo llegase a comprenderla, cuál es "la verdad de la milanesa".

TARAGÜI ÑE'É

El día en que los primeros soldados aliados desembarcaban en Sicilia en 1943, Gigí Musumeci padecía su segunda crisis de paludismo y no pudo celebrar la liberación. No sería el primero, ya que más de diez mil soldados americanos sufrieron una suerte similar en los pantanos de la región de Catania, notorio hábitat de los mosquitos anofeles. Las bajas fueron superiores a las heridas de guerra, sin contar las pérdidas causadas por el dengue y la fiebre de Malta. En esos tiempos era difícil distinguir entre ellas, y los soldados las conocían como FUO, o fiebre de origen desconocido. Poco después, cansado de la guerra, de la malaria y, sobre todo, del hambre y la miseria, Gigí se exilió como tripulante en un barco de carga con destino a América del Sur y su primera escala fue en Buenos Aires. Buscando trabajo, y mal informado sobre la geografía Argentina, continuó subiendo el río Paraná en una lancha de provisiones para los pobladores ribereños, hasta terminar como pescador en la paupérrima provincia de Corrientes.

Gigí confiaba en manejarse bien en español, ya que conocía algunas palabras de ese origen en el dialecto siciliano. En cambio, sus contactos entre la gente sencilla y trabajadora, pero menos educada, muchos de origen indígena, hablaban sobre todo una lengua incomprensible que llamaban taragüí ñe'é. Luego supo que taragüí era el nombre guaraní para Corrientes, y que también significaba 'lagartija', un bicho rapidísimo, pero tímido, que pululaba sobre los muros blancos. Sus nuevos amigos le explicaron que entre indios hablaban sobre todo avañé'é, o sea, "el lenguaje humano", para diferenciarlo desde época inmemorial del karaíñé'é o "palabra de los señores", los odiados conquistadores. En ese medio indígena aprendió a comunicarse sobre todo en guaraní y nunca llegó a hablar bien el español, igual que muchos de sus nuevos vecinos. Le contaron que los pocos soldados llegados del Paraguay que fundaron Corrientes en 1588 procuraron evangelizar a los aborígenes y prohibir el uso del idioma local. Pero la superioridad numérica indígena en cambio obligó a los españoles a aprender la lengua guaraní. Aun así, utilizaban hispanismos para referirse a números, colores y parentescos.

Gracias a su experiencia como pescador, Gigí Musumeci pudo sobrevivir por años en la costa de los tumultuosos ríos Paraná y Paraguay, descubiertos en 1527 por Sebastián Gaboto, el navegante veneciano. Gigí disfrutaba de sus combates contra peces de río que podían ser enormes, especies de inigualable fuerza y espíritu de lucha como los dorados, surubíes y bogas. Pero jamás olvidó los tiempos de pesca en

Sicilia, el Mediterráneo y el día glorioso de "la Tonnara", el 23 de abril, entre las islas de Favignana y Levanzo, en que el mar se cubre de rojo con la sangre de los atunes masacrados a palos. Las "matanzas" del atún solo habían enriquecido a muchos nobles sicilianos, pero estas memorias reconfortaban ahora a Gigí en su exilio correntino.

Se adaptó pronto a su nuevo medio, porque la fuerte religiosidad y el culto a los santos le recordaban su región natal. La cultura conservadora se asentaba en un componente mágico. Así encontró, en muchos caminos urbanos y rurales, unos altares adornados con banderas y cintas rojas, junto a la foto de un gaucho muy joven, posible víctima de una muerte violenta e injusta. Le explicaron que se trataba del "Gauchito Gil", un santo popular considerado milagroso, objeto de enorme devoción popular en esa zona. Aceptó como suya esta creencia y tenía un pequeño altar con cintas rojas en su propio rancho. Un 8 de enero, el día del aniversario del santo, visitó en la ciudad de Mercedes su santuario principal junto a cientos de miles de peregrinos para entregar ofrendas. Poco tiempo después de sus plegarias conoció a la mujer que sería su compañera en esas tierras.

Pescando por el Paraná, al norte de la capital provincial, se encontró en la ciudad costera de Itatí, coincidiendo con la fiesta de su virgen, el 16 de julio. A pesar de la muchedumbre, un anochecer consiguió sentarse a rezar en la basílica, vecino a una joven indígena, quien le sonrió, con un saludo en guaraní usado específicamente luego de la caída del sol:

—*¿Mbá eichapá nde pyharé?* (¿Cómo estás esta noche?)

Para entonces conocía bien la respuesta tradicional:

—*Che pyharé porã, ¿ha ndé?* (Muy bien. ¿Y tú?)

—*Che pyharé porã avei.* (Igualmente, gracias.)

Su nombre era Itatí, como el de la virgen de la basílica. Siguieron la charla en español, mezclado con bastantes palabras en guaraní. Gigí le contó sobre su exilio de Sicilia, su profesión de pescador y escuchó con interés algunos detalles sobre la vida de ella en una aldea cercana, en donde casualmente sus parientes eran también pescadores. Al rato de intercambiar comentarios, Itatí le invitó, inesperadamente, a un baile de pueblo:

—*¿Ejerókisé chendivé?* (¿Te gustaría bailar?)

Gigí, sorprendido, aceptó acompañarla a la fiesta en una cantina cercana, con un patio arbolado en donde músicos ambulantes con acordeón y guitarras tocaban alegremente un chamamé, una música folclórica muy rítmica y fluida, con cadencias que sugerían el correr del río Paraná. También improvisaban otros motivos de origen colonial con influencias europeas, como la polca correntina y el valseado. Los tonos del acordeón le recordaron la vieja música de su pueblo en Sicilia, y acrecentaron su afinidad por esta gente y sus costumbres.

Itatí resultó ser buena bailarina, espontánea y natural. Cautivado por su personalidad, volvió a ese pueblo varias veces, y eventualmente compró un ranchito frente al río para instalarse en la región y para vivir juntos. Estaba cerca de la zona que había elegido para la pesca, y el inconveniente principal eran las hordas de mosquitos que los afectaban cada anochecer, típicos de los trópicos. Itatí mezclaba unos ungüentos para protegerse un poco de las picaduras, como para suavizar la picazón. Pero la presencia de los insectos le producía pesadillas en que recordaba su lejana patria y los pantanos de Catania que hubiese querido dejar atrás.

Itatí era muy buena cocinera y dominaba los platos locales con maestría, especialmente los de pescado fresco, dorados o surubíes, cuando los traía su compañero luego de una exitosa jornada de pesca. En los anocheceres cálidos lo esperaba con un tereré helado, o con el mate bien cebado, gigantesco como un melón, la calabaza que les gusta usar también en el vecino Paraguay, al otro lado del río. Con frecuencia los acompañaba con tortas fritas, o chipacueritos, como le dicen en Corrientes, hechas con harina y grasa de vaca. En días de fiesta le preparaba el *mbeyú*, que en lengua guaraní significa 'torta aplastada', un manjar autóctono a base de almidón de mandioca, cuyos orígenes se remontan a las cocinas de las reducciones franciscanas y a las misiones jesuíticas.

A Gigí le encantaba pescar en el Paraná, y las batallas épicas con los enormes dorados, grandes luchadores. Su destreza fue recompensada por los indígenas de la zona, quienes lo apodaban "Parí", un experto en atrapar peces con los métodos guaraníes respetando el medio ambiente. Pero también pasaba mucho tiempo en la región pantanosa e insalubre de los Esteros del Iberá, en donde se encontraba con una fauna de todo tipo: mamíferos, reptiles, batracios, peces y, sobre todo, insectos. A veces atrapaba anguilas, tan sabrosas para los entendidos, y gozaba al pescar los tamboatás, pescaditos de unos seis centímetros de largo, porque eran grandes consumidores de mosquitos. Pero nunca se acostumbró a coexistir con las serpientes locales, las temidas yarará o víbora de la cruz, o las de coral multicolores, que a veces acababan con los lugareños y pescadores. En cambio se regocijaba rodeado de tantas aves, el tucán grande, el ñandú, los flamencos y teros, pájaros carpinteros y las coloridas cotorras. Esto disminuía su ansiedad y las pesadillas provocadas por los insectos, víboras y caimanes.

Al año de conocerse, Itatí dio a luz a una bella indiecita que llamaron Yrasema, como el "rumor del río", aunque sus amiguitas la apodaron Inés, nombre más fácil de pronunciar. Creció en la aldea sobre todo con la familia de su madre. Curiosamente, los genes sicilianos revelaron en su adolescencia un aspecto algo europeo, y cabellos castaño claro, con ojos profundamente negros. Le encantaba imitar los gestos de Gigí, quien hablaba mucho con las manos, y acompañarlo a veces en sus jornadas de pesca. Igual que su madre, hablaba de preferencia en guaraní, aunque entendía bastante español, se manejaba sin dificultades en la escuela y aprendió a leer y a escribir con facilidad. Sus padres la enviaron al colegio secundario en la ciudad de Corrientes, más populosa y desarrollada, ya que allí podía alojarse con sus tías y ayudarlas en la casa luego de la escuela. La aceptaron porque Gigí contribuía con un estipendio mensual, aunque sus ganancias eran muy limitadas y apenas alcanzaban para la subsistencia con su mujer.

El colegio secundario hizo que Inés conociera a gentes diversas y adquiriera nuevos amigos entre los extranjeros refugiados durante o después de la Segunda Guerra Mundial. Cuando una alumna de origen alemán se enfermó y dejó de asistir a clases, hubo rumores de que la atendía en un sitio remoto y secreto un "doctor" alemán que estaba protegido por el presidente Stroessner en el vecino Paraguay. Nunca imaginó que años más tarde confirmarían que había sido el notorio Dr. Mengele, el criminal de Auschwitz. Irónicamente, Inés conoció también a otros alemanes de origen judío, hijos y nietos de sobrevivientes de la guerra. Era la primera vez que ella escuchaba la palabra "judíos" y comprendió que alguna gente pertenecía a otras religiones distintas a la católica. Así se acercó a una alumna muy estudiosa, Ruth Goldman, para preparar exámenes juntas en su casa.

Algunas veces, luego de la práctica, la invitaban a quedarse para almorzar. Sus lazos se fueron reforzando durante sus caminatas juntas al atardecer alrededor de la plaza principal, un paseo conocido como la "vuelta del perro". Progresivamente el mundo de Yrasema se fue expandiendo, y descubrió que en la ciudad había otras minorías evangélicas y protestantes. La colectividad judía se congregaba en una sinagoga del centro y en la asociación cultural "Scholem Aleijem". Tenían un sitio para pícnics vecino al río, al cual Ruth la invitó algún domingo en que pudo conocer a otros miembros de la familia.

Una vez Ruth mencionó casualmente que no iban a poder encontrarse por unos días para la caminata juntas, porque su familia celebraba Pesach, las "Pascuas judías", que ese año eran unos días antes que las cristianas. Iba a ayudar a su madre a preparar un plato tradicional, un pescado relleno que ellos llamaban gefilte fish, hecho con pescados blancos, de preferencia carpa, como en Europa, y el pejerrey. Al escuchar las razones de Ruth, a Yrasema se le prendió una lamparita, una idea para corresponder a las amabilidades de sus nuevos amigos, entre los cuales se sentía tan aceptada. Entonces mandó pedir a Gigí que le hiciera llegar unos pescados frescos para regalarles el día siguiente, cuando su tío debería traer la pesca al mercado central. Así fue, y pudo entregárselos a Ruth muy orgullosa. El gefilte fish resultó excelente, y dijeron que fue "la mejor provisión de pescados que consiguieran desde su llegada al país".

Ese período de calma y felicidad, cuando Inés casi terminaba su secundaria, duró solo un corto tiempo. Por esa época veía poco a su padre, quien trabajaba mucho en la zona pantanosa plagada de mosquitos en el Iberá. Lo que siempre temía Gigí en sus pesadillas, la sorpresa de una nueva crisis de malaria, lo atacó de modo fulminante. Posiblemente esta vez fuera causada por el Plasmodium falciparum, diferente y más grave que el P. Vivax que lo había afectado en Sicilia en su juventud. En pocas horas empeoró con síntomas cerebrales, cayó en un coma profundo y lo trasladaron al hospital central de Corrientes, en donde solo tenían quinina para tratar la fiebre.

Cuando habían pasado unos quince años desde su llegada a Corrientes, Gigí sucumbió a un ataque final de paludismo, endémico en la provincia que lo había acogido durante la guerra.

Esta gran tragedia transformó drásticamente las vidas de Inés y de Itatí, quien quedó sin recursos para mantener a su hija. Sin las contribuciones de Gigí, las tías de Inés ya no tenían incentivo para recibirla. En poco tiempo dejó la escuela y se vio reducida a buscar empleo como doméstica, porque las oportunidades de trabajo para una joven indígena en el alto Paraná eran casi inexistentes.

Transcurrían las semanas, mientras Inés, a pesar de su carácter optimista y risueño, caía poco a poco en la depresión. Hasta que, en una mañana soleada del sábado, en que no trabajaba, se presentó sorpresivamente su amiga Ruth:

—*Maitei,* Inés, querida, ¿*Mba Eichapá?*

—*Maitei,* Ruth, es terrible. Ando con muchas dificultades económicas y estoy triste por no poder seguir estudiando.

—Lo siento mucho, pero vengo con una idea que podría ayudarte.

—No creo, Ruth, no hay nada que hacer —respondió desesperada.

—Claro que hay. Mirá, quiero invitarte mañana mismo al pícnic de la asociación cultural. Es urgente que vengas a conocer a unos amigos que nos visitan de Buenos Aires. Es importante presentarte bien vestida. Yo te vendría a buscar en el auto de papá, el poderoso Ford 39 que él me permite manejar, y como sabrás esto es inusitado para una chica acá en provincia. ¡Vamos a entrar como dos reinas! Hay que impresionar bien a estos turistas.

Ya en el pícnic, Inés notó que la miraban más que de costumbre, sobre todo una pareja de gente ya grande, que no parecían argentinos, y que no dejaban de estudiarla con intensidad. Finalmente, la mamá de Ruth la tomó de un brazo para presentarla a sus amigos.

—Hola, Inés. Somos de Buenos Aires, viejos amigos de la familia. Nos han hablado muy bien de vos, dicen que sos compañera de Ruth del secundario y que estudias muy bien. ¿Nunca estuviste en la capital?

—No, señora, solo conozco Corrientes. Vivo acá desde que falleció papá.

—¿Qué tal te llevás con gente grande, y con los que no hablan bien en español?

—Me encantan los grandes, como mi abuelita y sus hermanas. Además con Ruth estoy acostumbrada a estar con inmigrantes europeos.

—Bueno, qué te parecería venir a Buenos Aires para acompañar a una señora grande de Rusia, que necesita que la ayuden en la casa para hacer las compras y un poquito de limpieza y, sobre todo, para que no esté sola mientras su marido trabaja. Son de toda confianza y buena gente. Los papás de Ruth se hacen responsables por vos, te conocen bien. Allí tienen lugar para otra persona, estarías muy cómoda. Te pueden dar casa y comida, además de un pequeño sueldo para economizar, o mandarle a tu mamá si es necesario. Si ella está de acuerdo, podríamos llevarte con nosotros en el auto, en pocos días, al terminar nuestras excursiones por acá. ¿Qué te parece?

Inés la miró con asombro, desconcertada por esta posibilidad de escape inimaginable. Si su madre la dejara ir, aceptaría de inmediato. Solo lamentaría dejarla sola, y alejarse de su mejor amiga, pero pensó poder adaptarse a esta aventura inesperada. Corrió de inmediato a explicarle la idea a Itatí, quien no tuvo más remedio que acceder, con gran dolor, pero llena de esperanza por su hija. Pocos días más tarde, Yrasema partía hacia el sur desconocido y una nueva vida en la capital.

***

El día en que la conocí, yo venía de mi colegio secundario a almorzar en casa de mi abuela, quien me había prometido unas milanesas de ternera. Pero no me había anunciado que iba a compartirlas con una desconocida. Al tope de la escalera, en el pequeño patio de entrada frente a la minúscula cocina, me encontré con una jovencita de mi edad que me observaba con curiosidad. Sabía ya algunas cosas sobre mí, pero yo no tenía idea de su existencia. Sus primeras palabras me asombraron tanto como su presencia allí:

—*Maité*, Armando, ¿*Mbá Eichapá*?

—Hola. Disculpame, no te entiendo una palabra. ¿Estás de visita?

—Perdoname, por costumbre te saludé en guaraní. Soy Inés, la nueva compañera de la señora Lita. Voy a vivir con tus abuelos. ¡Mucho gusto!

Ese día la dejaron sentar con nosotros, pero en

general comía en la cocina cuando mis abuelos y otros familiares estábamos en el living. Su presencia constante me desconcertó, pero no temí que me fuera a reemplazar en el afecto incondicional de mis abuelos. Nunca llegué a conocerla bien, ya que comencé pronto a estudiar en la Facultad de Medicina, seis años de cursos, y tenía pocas ocasiones para visitarlos durante el día. Supe que se llevaban bien, que era amable y servicial y que, poco a poco, se transformó en una compañera inestimable para Lita, especialmente luego del fallecimiento de su marido, unos pocos años más tarde. Se llevaba bien con mi prima Patricia, quien tenía unos pocos años menos, y pasaban bastante tiempo juntas. Yo tenía poco contacto con Inés, en parte porque compartíamos distintos intereses con mis amigos de la facultad. Además, desde que tuve mi primera novia, me quedaba menos tiempo para estar con la familia. Al terminar el internado en medicina, dejé el país para radicarme y estudiar en los Estados Unidos. Ese fue nuestro último encuentro con la joven correntina, ¡ya que nunca volvimos a vernos en los próximos cincuenta años!

Ahora, una vida más tarde y en Seattle, mi ciudad predilecta, algunas memorias que ignoraba que se habían infiltrado en el inconsciente han vuelto a aparecer como por casualidad, tanto tiempo después. Ocurrió que hace pocos días recibí una llamada de Patricia por WhatsApp desde Buenos Aires, para saludarme por mi cumpleaños:

—¡Qué bueno encontrarte para tu cumple, primo! Ya vamos quedando pocos para llamarte desde acá. Un abrazo de mi hermano y su señora, y un gran saludo de alguien con quien acabo de hablar por teléfono. ¿Te acordás de Inés, la compañera de Lita? Cuando hablamos hace poco me pidió muchísimo que te salude de su parte. Quiere saber si todavía te gusta pescar, y si usas el método que ella te había enseñado. La mención de la pesca me puso la carne de gallina. Me trajo de vuelta aquel día de verano, con 35 grados a la sombra, en que participé por primera vez en un concurso de pesca en la Costanera del Río de la Plata.

No tenía experiencia ni ningún equipo, excepto el que me preparó Inés con su sabiduría correntina, producto de sus años jóvenes en el río Paraná, con su familia de pescadores y su papá, Gigí.

—Vamos a la ferretería a comprar una línea de nailon, una cucharita plateada, una plomada livianita y un anzuelo. El resto lo tenemos en la cocina —me explicó, mientras abría y vaciaba una lata de duraznos en almíbar, le hacía un agujerito con un clavo para pasar la línea y atarla por dentro con un palito—. Con esto te ganás el campeonato, porque vas a sacar más bagres que nadie. Yo te muestro cómo se hace cuando lleguemos al río.

Su técnica magistral se reveló de inmediato, ya que podía revolear y tirar el anzuelo más lejos que muchos en la Costanera y, en pocos minutos, ¡con ese método primitivo, pude sacar mi primer bagre! No gané el campeonato, pero me divertí mucho y sigo utilizando esa habilidad hasta el día de hoy. ¡Me sirvió para pescar desde mi kayak un sabroso salmón de varias libras en las aguas frías de la Columbia Británica, con gran asombro de los canadienses bien equipados que observaban incrédulos mi baratísima técnica correntina!

Pocos días más tarde me comuniqué nuevamente con Patricia quien, entretanto, había reflexionado sobre otros incidentes.

—Yo también me acuerdo de cosas que hacíamos juntas —me dijo, algo emocionada—. Nos gustaba sentarnos por la tarde con Inés en la cocinita para escuchar radionovelas con una radio de galena.

—¿Una radio de galena? No te puedo creer, nadie usaba semejante antigüedad. Ya había buenos equipos electrónicos y televisión para entonces.

—Así fue, pero no nos dejaban usar el estéreo y el tocadiscos que había en el comedor. La de galena la había comprado el abuelo Lito al llegar de Palestina y de algún modo todavía estaba en la cocina. Solo se escuchaba muy bajito y sintonizaba una o dos estaciones. Había que mover la posición de una aguja sobre la piedra de galena para encontrar algún programa. Pero también podíamos escuchar una audición folclórica que le encantaba, porque a veces pasaban música correntina y de tango, que llegó a gustarle bastante. Ahora tiene un hijo al que le dio por ese lado.

—¿No la dejaban salir con amigos los fines de semana? —pregunté por curiosidad.

—Por supuesto, cuando creció un poco salía con otras chicas del barrio a bailar en Palermo, en un sitio que tocaban mucho chamamé, y eso la transportaba a su provincia natal. En esos bailes conoció a su futuro marido, un italiano del sur con quien tuvo dos hijos varones. ¡No lo vas a creer! A uno le puso de nombre Enrique, como el abuelo, y al otro lo llamó Marcelo, en honor a tu papá, a quien apreciaba mucho porque la trataba como a una hija. Ahora casi no la veo a Inés, está bastante anciana y no nos visita ni llama tanto. No sabría cómo hacer para que puedas hablarle. Pero me enteré de que Marcelo es un cantor de tango muy conocido.

—¡Eso me interesa! Como sabrás, el tango es una de mis pasiones. Me gustaría comunicarme con él, quizá nos ponga en contacto con su madre. ¿Sabés cómo encontrarlo?

—Solamente te puedo decir que se hace llamar "Facundo Catania" en su trabajo.

—Voy a buscarlo y veremos si me ayuda. Yo quisiera escribir sobre la vida de Inés antes de venir a la capital, ya que solo conozco lo que nos habían contado los paisanos amigos que la trajeron a casa de los abuelos. Ellos habían hablado bastante con la familia que la recomendó. Pero me gustaría profundizar en la influencia indígena y también la de su padre siciliano en Corrientes. Al principio, Inés se confundía y a veces hablaba en guaraní. Por entonces yo tenía otras preocupaciones, y nunca me interesé en saber más detalles. Pero, ahora que me interesa la escritura, sería fascinante entender su experiencia antes de que la conociéramos.

Hoy en día es muy difícil esconderse sin dejar rastros, ni de la policía, ni de investigadores privados, o simplemente de los algoritmos de los grandes medios sociales. No era la primera vez que localizaba a gente en forma inesperada gracias al internet, los que terminaban como personajes en alguno de mis relatos. En este caso, luego de pocos minutos de búsqueda, descubrí un anuncio sobre un espectáculo de tango en el café Homero Manzi, en la esquina de Boedo y San Juan, a dos cuadras del antiguo domicilio de mis abuelos cuando yo era joven. El cantante del grupo era un tal Facundo Catania y tenía una página en Facebook y un número de contacto en WhatsApp, que me respondió de inmediato.

—¿Estás llamando desde Estados Unidos?

—Así es, mi nombre es Armando y conozco desde joven a tu madre, Inés, de cuando vivía en casa de mis abuelos. No la vi nunca más desde que dejé el país hace cincuenta años. Me gustaría poder hablarle para rememorar tiempos viejos.

—Por supuesto, yo sé de quién se trata. Mi hermano y yo conocemos muy bien a tu familia, que mamá quiere tanto, y especialmente conocimos a tus padres, que la trataban tan bien. ¡Increíble, tengo que llamar a Inés para contarle! Mejor hagamos así: la voy a ver ya mismo en la residencia geriátrica que queda cerca y la dejo hablarte con mi celular, así se comunican directamente. Esperá una llamada mía de acá en quince minutos.

Al poco rato sonó el teléfono y hablamos con Inés como si "cincuenta años no es nada", parafraseando la letra del tango "Volver".

—¡Armando! no puedo creer que estemos hablando y que todavía te acuerdes de mí. ¡Qué bueno que hayas conversado un poco con mi hijo Marcelo, que se llama igual que tu papá! Extraño mucho a tus padres y a los abuelos. Aun me acuerdo cuando venías a almorzar desde el colegio o de la facultad. Tu abuela te hacía tus comidas favoritas, que yo aprendí a preparar. ¿Podés creer que hasta el día de hoy puedo hacer prakes, los rollos de repollo rellenos con carne picada? y los latkes de papa, que a mis hijos también les encantan. Debo ser la única correntina que sepa hacer un buenísimo gefilte fish, y que entienda algunas palabras en yidish. —Lo curioso es que mientras me comentaba sobre sus habilidades en la cocina con estas recetas judías, se escuchaba una música de fondo que era indudablemente un chamamé.

—Por mi lado, te cuento que seguimos casados con Diana, a quien conociste, tenemos un hijo médico como nosotros y dos nietos. Pero más te va a gustar saber que sigo pescando con una lata de duraznos en almíbar como vos me enseñaste cuando yo era todavía un estudiante. Tenías razón en que si la lata es de durazno y no de otra fruta, parece dar mejores resultados. Inés, me gustaría que me cuentes algo sobre tu vida antes de llegar a la capital, cuando vivías en Corrientes y hablabas el guaraní, como tu familia. ¿Te acordás de esas cosas? Al menos observo que te sigue gustando el chamamé, y que lo estabas escuchando recién.

—De eso no quiero hablar, y mis hijos tampoco conocen esos detalles. Todo eso está olvidado, y no recuerdo ni una palabra que no sea en español. Pero ahora me viene a la mente lo de la pesca, como me dijiste. Yo era buena para eso. Mejor hablemos de mi vida actual. Te cuento que con mi marido teníamos una mercería hasta hace poco. Él es italiano, igual que mi papá Gigí. Nuestros hijos son ítalo-argentinos, como muchos de por acá, y Marcelo, bueno, ahora le gusta más llamarse Facundo, es un cantor de tango bastante popular. Tiene un espectáculo en el barrio de tus abuelos, en que yo también crecí. Pero ahora no puedo hablar mucho, me canso y mejor que te lo pase de nuevo a él, que te contará otras cosas. Mejor que vuelvas a llamar otro día. Un abrazo, y espero que nos visites pronto.

Fue lindo escuchar su voz y rememorar un poco, aunque me decepcionó mucho que no recordase, o no quisiera mencionar detalles, sobre su juventud con Marcelo presente. Tampoco le había dicho mucho a sus hijos, que parecían conocer mejor la comida judía que la de Corrientes. Era obvio que la vida había sido muy dura en aquellos tiempos y que había preferido dejarla atrás. Mis opciones para recabar más datos se habían derrumbado súbitamente. Parecía claro que no iba a conocer más detalles y que su juventud quedaría esfumada en una nube de misterio.

Así lo reconoció Marcelo, cuando se puso otra vez al teléfono:

—Mamá es muy buena cocinera, y muchas de las recetas las aprendió de tu abuela Lita. Lo raro es que ahora no le apetece mucho comer pescado. No sé si será porque los de acá en la capital no siempre son frescos como a ella le gustan, o porque no quiere acordarse de algunas cosas que nunca nos contó.

—Marcelo, o si preferís, Facundo — le dije —,

voy a tener que despedirme por el momento. Vos y yo tenemos en común el que haya conocido a tu madre cuando joven, además de ser un viejo milonguero, y que me apasiona el tango como a vos. Por eso, quisiera escuchar tu música. ¿Podrías mandarla en un archivo adjunto?

—Perfecto, te hago escuchar las de mis mejores éxitos. Después me darás tu opinión.

—Mientras hablábamos con Inés, se oía una música de fondo que me resultó conocida. Aunque ella dice no acordarse de su juventud en Corrientes, lo que estaba escuchando era un chamamé. Es evidente que le sigue gustando. Bueno, Facundo, quedemos en contacto, y ya sea los visito un día en Buenos Aires, o mejor aún, quizá podamos coordinar una visita tuya a Estados Unidos para cantar en una de nuestras milongas en Seattle. Entre tanto, ¡un abrazo para los dos!

Curiosamente, mi redescubrimiento de Corrientes, su gente y su música se revelaron proféticos. Al corregir este manuscrito, Lupe, la editora madrileña de estos cuentos en español, me comentó con unas palabras que estoy obligado a compartir ahora:

"Estimado Armando:

No sé si le he contado alguna vez que soy gran amante del chamamé y me gusta mucho este músico, acordeonista, Chango Spasiuk. Seguramente usted lo conozca. Vino hace no mucho a tocar a Madrid. Alejandro, mi pareja, fue a verlo. Le mando un vídeo sobre él donde cuenta que (desde el 2020) el chamamé fue declarado por la Unesco patrimonio inmaterial de la Humanidad. Yo también vibro con el chamamé".

VUDÚ

El distanciamiento social y los cierres de 2020 nos han transformado a los que éramos sociables. De pronto nos sentimos incómodos con otra gente. Nuestra elocuencia está oxidada, extrañamos la conversación, los placeres de la vida urbana callejera y los encuentros casuales. A la vez, agradezco haber tenido tiempo para la autorreflexión. Esto me está permitiendo revivir sentimientos olvidados, como una tendencia latente hacia la superstición y la magia. Así, en una tarde perezosa, recordé que un día había recurrido al vudú para hacerle daño a una enemiga.

Algunos amigos que me conocen bien se han preguntado cómo era posible que yo, un médico serio, un investigador crítico, albergara al mismo tiempo pensamientos negros y una especulación extravagante.

Mi interés por temas arcanos, como la filosofía espiritual, se desarrolló durante los años 60, en el momento en que Louis Pauwels, un periodista, y Jacques Bergier, un ingeniero químico, publicaron en Francia

El retorno de los brujos, que se convirtió en un libro de culto internacional entre los jóvenes. Curiosamente, Bergier —nacido Yakov Mikhailovich Berger, en Odesa, no muy lejos de algunos de mis antepasados— también fue un espía de la Resistencia francesa en Lyon, como mi tío Nathan. Bergier fue un erudito en el Talmud y la Cábala, la historia prohibida y el ocultismo. Sus antecedentes e intereses lo hicieron muy atractivo para mí. Sin embargo, yo era consciente de que los autores habían declarado que «[...] en nuestro libro habrá un montón de tonterías, pero eso no tiene importancia si estimula algunas vocaciones nuevas». Por cierto, su publicación influyó en parte en el desarrollo de mi personalidad y, quizá, en la idea subconsciente de querer aplicar el vudú en un futuro lejano.

En una noche de insomnio debido a la pandemia, recordé un encuentro azaroso que tuve muchos años atrás, durante unas vacaciones en el balneario de Mar del Plata, en Argentina. Una tarde, agotado después de una larga caminata, sentí que una atracción casi magnética me arrastraba hacia un banco en un parque de la ciudad. Tuve que compartir el único asiento disponible con un hombre ya grande, rodeado por un aura oscura. Me escudriñó con una mirada tan penetrante como una radiografía de hueso. La portada del libro que tenía en mi regazo encendió su curiosidad y, de pronto, dijo:

—Usted es un médico judío, ¿no es cierto?

—¡Así es! ¿Cómo puede haberlo adivinado?

—Bueno, puedo ver cosas. Conozco bien este libro. ¿Qué lo impulsó a leerlo?

—Lo estoy leyendo por segunda vez, porque es entretenido y pseudocientífico. Trata de temas extraños, inusuales, es ideal para unas vacaciones.

—Dice que es entretenido, pero compruebo que ha releído varias veces la teoría de un próximo salto evolutivo en la conciencia humana que resultará en un hombre nuevo. ¿Por qué le fascina? ¿Se considera una de esas mutaciones?

—Por supuesto que no, eso es pura especulación. Pero ¿cómo pudo saber que estoy leyendo ese capítulo? No nos conocemos ni hemos hablado hasta ahora.

El libro estaba cerrado y sin signos externos, como un marcador de página, que indicaran el capítulo o la página que repasaba.

—Como le dije, soy clarividente. Usted me hace visualizar a Nostradamus, otro médico judío de la Edad Media, quien podía predecir el futuro. ¿Ha oído hablar de él?

—Claro que sí. Nostradamus era francés, como mi padre, y vivía en Saint-Rémy de Provence, donde tuve ocasión de visitar su museo. Pero las investigaciones serias han desacreditado sus profecías. Es una buena diversión, pero pura charlatanería.

—No debería ser tan escéptico. En todo caso, ¿por qué está leyendo ese libro?

Expuesto a su inexplicable intuición, cada minuto me notaba más intranquilo. Tenía algo misterioso, quizá maligno, como si lo rodeara un campo energético.

—¿Cómo puede probar que es clarividente?

—No necesito probarlo. Prefiero ayudarlo a visualizar sus propios poderes. Por ejemplo, escriba el nombre de una persona en un papel, dóblelo bien y démelo.

Sentía que era el momento de escapar, recordando la expresión «la curiosidad mató al gato». Sin embargo, no podía retirarme sin comprender un poco mejor con quién estaba. Por eso garabateé lo primero que se me ocurrió: el nombre de alguien con una historia familiar trágica, un viejo amigo de mi padre. El hombre me quitó el papel, lo cubrió con ambas manos y cerró los ojos en actitud de concentración durante casi un minuto, antes de manifestar en tono grave:

—Lo que veo es muy inquietante. Está borroso, espere un momento. Veo a una niña pequeña que estaba en una foto en el diario hace bastantes años. ¿De qué se trata? Es algo horrible, una tragedia. ¿Cómo la conoció usted?

Su comentario me horrorizó. Sus facultades sobrepasaban todas mis experiencias anteriores. Me había convencido de su clarividencia.

—No entiendo cómo lo hace, pero confieso que usted ha descubierto nuevamente lo que estaba pensando. La hermanita de este hombre fue víctima de un asesino en serie hace bastante tiempo. Fue capturado y lo mandaron a la colonia penal de máxima seguridad en Ushuaia. ¿Cómo pudo saber tanto al respecto con solo un nombre que usted no tuvo posibilidad de leer?

Su demostración resultó aterradora, y hasta espeluznante.

Me levanté, decidido a irme, pero él me detuvo con un brazo extendido, antes de añadir un último comentario:

—¡Usted posee poderes similares! Los sentí apenas se acercó a este banco, solo que usted no tiene conciencia de ellos. Debería comprender su propia energía y aprender a usarla. Con el tiempo, descubrirá que puede hacer otras cosas con su mente, cuando aprenda a controlarla. Voy a predecir que un día va a ser capaz de herir a un enemigo con solo desearle daño. Nos parecemos mucho. Adiós, y recuerde mis palabras.

Su capacidad y su visión sobre mi futuro me horrorizaron.

Me fui corriendo sin mirar atrás ni planear volver a verlo nunca. Sin embargo, creo que relegué este encuentro a algún rincón oscuro de mi subconsciente.

Mis defensas psicológicas no me permiten evocar a menudo esa reunión dantesca, pero, en cambio, reconozco mi tendencia a otros temores y a pensamientos mórbidos. Por ejemplo, una vez, durante un viaje familiar a Bali, hace unos treinta años, una tormenta tropical y lluvias torrenciales nos obligaron a refugiarnos en una rústica casa de té. Como es costumbre en este país, la puerta de entrada apuntaba hacia el lado del mar o hacia el poniente. Apenas cruzada la puerta, reconocí un mal augurio, un biombo de bambú nos forzaba a un cambio de dirección alrededor del muro, para disuadir la entrada a los espíritus maléficos.

Mi esposa, Diana, Serge, mi hijo y yo habíamos

compartido mesa con un grupo de jóvenes holandeses, en un patio con techo de bambú, sin paredes, abierto hacia un camino fangoso. El atardecer y la oscuridad se presentaron repentinamente, como ocurre cerca del ecuador. Entonces nos envolvió una niebla teatral, realzada por la iluminación romántica de las suaves luces de las velas. La música hipnótica de un gamelán se batía en conflicto con el violento sonajero de la lluvia sobre la vegetación exterior. Mientras charlábamos en tono bajo con nuestros vecinos, la escena me recordaba algún cuento de Edgar Allan Poe.

La entrada de un murciélago rompió ese momento casi místico. Era del tamaño de un perro pequeño y comenzó a girar por encima de nuestras cabezas, mientras se mantenía alejado de las otras personas. El animal volaba más y más rápido, formando círculos cada vez más cerrados, hasta casi rozar nuestras cabezas. Admito que éramos suburbanitas poco acostumbrados a los animales salvajes, pequeños o grandes, en nuestras inmediaciones. Nuestros compañeros del momento parecían impertérritos. Sin embargo, la sensación era ominosa. ¿Por qué volaba justo sobre nuestro pequeño grupo y evitaba a los demás? ¿Cómo podía distinguirnos tan bien con la débil luz de las velas? ¿Sería un murciélago carnívoro y quizá rabioso? Presa de un miedo incontrolable, dejé dinero sobre la mesa para pagar la cuenta y, con la familia, abandonamos el barco en desgracia. Preferí hacer frente a la tormenta en la sombría carretera secundaria. Aunque el murciélago no nos había seguido, la aprehensión persistió hasta que entramos en nuestra cabaña, situada a una milla de camino. Mientras nos alejábamos del local, la lluvia se disipó poco a poco y los cielos se fueron abriendo progresivamente hasta que un número infinito de estrellas brilló en el firmamento más negro que habíamos visto.

Incluso hoy, años después, la incertidumbre de la pandemia y la falta de control sobre una situación desconocida despertaron ese sentimiento de temor ante lo extraño y lo imprevisto.

A la mañana siguiente, me desperté con la premonición de que el día traería un cambio positivo que iba a romper el ciclo de temor. Esta percepción estaba justificada, ya que dio lugar a una experiencia propicia que tendría consecuencias fundamentales.

Después del desayuno, teníamos en mente un recorrido por la isla, interesados en visitar aldeas, buscando la oportunidad fotográfica. Necesitaba un taxi y confiaba en elegir al mejor conductor entre los que se encontraban en las inmediaciones del hotel. Mientras escaneaba el campo, uno de ellos, un hombre delgado de mediana edad, con una expresión pacífica, salió de su coche. Casi simultáneamente, como por telepatía, tomamos una decisión clarísima: él tenía que ser nuestro chófer.

Ya de excursión, pasamos por una plantación de arroz con una casa de paredes amarillas, rodeada de exuberantes flores rojas desconocidas para mí. Atraído por el colorido contraste, le pedí al conductor que se detuviera, pues quería fotografiar ese encantador entorno. Decidí enfocar selectivamente sobre una flor en particular, dejando que la casa, situada al fondo, quedara borrosa. A mi espalda, el conductor observaba silenciosamente mi tarea. Cuando terminé, me interrogó con diplomacia en un inglés lento, pero educado.

—Perdóneme, señor, ¿podría preguntarle por qué tomó esa fotografía?

—¡Cómo no! —contesté, perplejo—. Vivo en un país del norte con una vegetación muy diferente, donde no hay plantas tropicales como estas. Me gustó el fuerte contraste de color entre las flores y la pintura de la casa.

—Ya veo, pero, disculpe de nuevo, señor, ¿dónde está el elemento humano?

Esta observación pertinente me dejó mudo. Durante el resto de la gira, la repetí en mi mente antes de disparar, en cada oportunidad fotográfica.

A continuación nos detuvimos en un pueblo donde dos hombres estaban entrenando sus gallos para una riña. El conductor les pidió permiso, en bahasa, para tomar fotos, y me agaché para fotografiar de cerca las expresiones de los hombres así como las de los gallos. Los paisanos me miraron con curiosidad, ya que éramos tan extraños los unos como los otros.

El ambiente tranquilo del pueblo y la ferocidad de los animales de riña me causaron una sensación surrealista que traté de reflejar en las imágenes. El conductor me observaba con interés, pero permaneció en silencio.

Por la noche, cuando regresamos al hotel, le pagué la cuenta al conductor, añadiendo una generosa propina. Ese fue mi turno de charlar con él:

—Esta mañana, la primera pregunta que usted hizo sobre mi elección de tema fue realmente instructiva. ¿Cómo sabe tanto sobre fotografía?

Con una brillante sonrisa y, sin otra palabra, sacó del bolsillo de su camisa una tarjeta de visita, que me presentó con evidente orgullo. Leí su nombre indonesio y un título: «Presidente de la Sociedad Balinesa de Fotografía».

Este encuentro inolvidable determinó el curso de mi vida como fotógrafo aficionado. Desde ese día, antes de tomar una instantánea, recuerdo esa profunda observación: «¿Dónde está el elemento humano?». Pero ahora, un montón de años después, a consecuencia de la pandemia y frustrado por el distanciamiento social, ya no puedo seguir el precepto de Robert Capa: «Si la imagen no funcionó, no estabas lo suficientemente cerca».

Normalmente llevo una cámara cada vez que salgo. En una ocasión, esto me ayudó a confirmar la proximidad de una enemiga en el trabajo. Un día, desde el alto mirador de la ventana de mi consulta en el hospital, admiraba los árboles de abajo, rodeados por una densa y misteriosa niebla. Una motocicleta se iba perdiendo en silencio en el estacionamiento para los pacientes. Tomé mi cámara para grabar esa escena casi cinematográfica. Mi puerta estaba abierta, como de costumbre, cuando una voz familiar detrás de mí criticó mi actividad:

—Veo que te sobra tiempo para jugar en el trabajo. ¡Y después te quejas de estar demasiado ocupado por tus casos clínicos!

Ese comentario era maligno y sumamente injusto, porque yo atendía a casi un centenar de pacientes. Mi colega, en cambio, gozaba de abundante tiempo libre para la investigación en el laboratorio. En ese momento, en nuestra Facultad de Medicina la atención al paciente y la investigación clínica eran bastante menos gratificantes que los trabajos de laboratorio.

A pesar de tener unas jornadas apretadas, en el intervalo disponible entre pacientes yo luchaba por producir datos en el laboratorio. Uno de mis proyectos había dado sólidos resultados preliminares y estaba ansioso por continuar. Esto requería el uso de isótopos radioactivos con una ventilación adecuada. Cuando le pedí permiso a mi colega para utilizar la campana del estudio que compartíamos, su respuesta no me sorprendió: «Lo siento, no puedo dejar que la uses. Como médico clínico, tienes menos experiencia en el laboratorio. Podrías contaminar el área y afectar nuestros resultados. Tendrás que encontrar una campana en otro sitio».

La respuesta era ridícula, ya que mi asistente era un bioquímico muy competente. Me vi obligado a buscar un lugar alternativo y colegas amistosos y decentes, con mejor disposición.

En especial, demostraba su antagonismo más feroz hacia otras mujeres que ella pensaba que podrían competir por los mismos objetivos. Era una mentirosa compulsiva y una experta en inflar su capacidad profesional. Aun con estos antecedentes, había presentado su candidatura como presidenta de la Sociedad Americana de Mujeres en Medicina. Con gran sorpresa y para mi consternación, su nombramiento fue aceptado.

Mi enemiga mostró su verdadera personalidad en una reunión del comité de promociones, al votar en contra de una de las profesoras más jóvenes, quien, claramente, merecía un ascenso. Allí fue evidente que la hipócrita colega ya había formado su opinión sobre este caso:

—Ella no está preparada para ser promovida. Sus publicaciones son de una calidad moderada y no muy imaginativas. Está sobrecargada de trabajo con sus pacientes y al ser mujer, tiene una familia, dos escolares que necesitan ayuda y una casa que cuidar. No creo que tenga posibilidades de éxito en nuestro difícil campo de investigación. Vamos a reconsiderar su caso en el futuro.

Lamentablemente, ella había reservado su oposición más agresiva en contra de mi ascenso, lo cual tuvo severas repercusiones en mi carrera.

Poco a poco, mi disgusto hacia ella se convirtió en odio. No necesitaba más pruebas. Como decía Woody Allen en una de sus comedias, estábamos de acuerdo en que «Incluso las personas paranoicas pueden tener enemigos». Lo único que no tenía claro era cómo tomar mi revancha. Para dar un golpe más contundente, necesitaría convocar fuerzas oscuras, más poderosas que las disponibles para ella.

Una posible venganza se me ocurrió casualmente mientras escuchaba afro-pop, ya que la música popular internacional es una de mis pasiones. En 2010, Haití debió sobrevivir a un terremoto, a una epidemia de cólera y al desorden político. Había quienes postulaban a su música como antídoto ante un océano de negatividad. En este trasfondo, un grupo de músicos formó Lakou Mizik, una espectacular banda rítmica que mezclaba elementos de los estilos *troubadou,* rara y rap. Luego agregaron el espíritu conmovedor de una iglesia negra y el trance inducido por los rituales del vudú. Escuchando a Lakou Mizik bajo la influencia de un poderoso ron haitiano, recordé las palabras de aquel clarividente hechicero que había conocido en Argentina cuando era joven. Comprendí que era hora de ejercitar mi mente contra las fuerzas de la oscuridad. Esto me obligó a estudiar las diferencias entre una ceremonia vudú y la religión *Vodou* (con V mayúscula), que, más que una creencia, es una forma de vida.

Entre 1791 y 1804, las prácticas vudú contribuyó a aumentar el poder de la población africana, lo que culminó en la expulsión de los franceses de Haití. Los colonos que sobrevivieron huyeron a Nueva Orleans, llevando con ellos a sus esclavos de habla francesa. Tanto la religión *Vodou* como las prácticas mágicas del vudú han sobrevivido en el fértil entorno de Nueva Orleans. ¡Y esto fue muy oportuno, ya esa ciudad era el destino de mi esposa para una conferencia de pediatría!

De modo que recluté a Diana para investigar el potencial de las prácticas haitianas como defensa contra mi malvada colega. Una vez allí, mi esposa se dio cuenta de que no tendría acceso a las auténticas congregaciones de vudú y sus templos para interactuar con sacerdotes y sacerdotisas, algunos de ellos iniciados en Haití. El visitante ocasional a Nueva Orleans solo encuentra tours sensacionalistas como «vudú y fantasmas» y tiendas de recuerdos especializadas en «vudú turístico». Sin embargo, en uno de estos establecimientos, Diana dio con un supuesto «doctor o reina» vudú. La propietaria empatizó mucho con el relato sobre mi colega y accedió a ungir una de las muñecas con poderes especiales durante un ritual que llevó a cabo en ese momento. Además, recomendó que primero yo meditara bajo un *mapou*, una ceiba sagrada, para convocar a los espíritus santos, como los practicantes de vudú.

Cuando Diana regresó a casa, fui, como me indicó la «reina», al jardín botánico para sentarme bajo un *mapou*. Después, abrí la caja para extraer una bonita figura negra con un vestido rojo y un pañuelo en la cabeza. Las instrucciones eran simples: «Adjuntar unos recortes de uñas o cabellos de la persona, el blanco deseado, y luego pinchar la muñeca con alfileres en el lugar donde prefiera infligir el daño». A pesar del dudoso origen de la muñeca, la superstición se apoderó de mí y decidí intentarlo. ¡Pensé que había encontrado la forma perfecta de vengarme! Nuestros despachos eran contiguos, así que una noche, mientras mi némesis estaba de viaje, recogí algunos cabellos de su sofá. Luego los fijé con alfileres en las piernas de la muñeca y la colgué detrás de la puerta de mi consulta, muy cerca de la suya. Con la puerta abierta, la muñeca no estaba visible. Entonces dirigí toda mi energía mental a lograr mi objetivo, esperando, con confianza, un resultado.

Por otro lado, estaba un poco avergonzado de mis métodos para ajustar viejas cuentas. Si mis amigos lo supieran, podría escuchar sus palabras escépticas resonando en mis oídos: «¿Esperabas que funcionara este truco infantil y supersticioso?».

En cambio sucedió que, exactamente veinticuatro horas después del regreso de mi enemiga a la consulta, se cayó por las escaleras cuando volvía a su casa por la noche y se rompió la pierna derecha en varios lugares. No podía moverse y tuvo que esperar en agonía durante varias horas hasta que el personal de mantenimiento la encontró. ¡El cirujano ortopédico del hospital necesitó implantarle grandes clavos en la tibia, cerca del lugar donde yo había colocado los alfileres en la muñeca!

Tuve buen cuidado de no proclamar que había deseado su mal y que había elegido muñecas vudú como instrumento de venganza. Pero un día, asombrado por el espectacular resultado, lo hablé confidencialmente con Marcel, mi amigo haitiano. Mientras se burlaba de mí, su pregunta era previsible:

—¿Cómo puedes probar una relación de causa-efecto? Cuesta creer que le hicieras daño a esa mujer jugando con una muñeca.

Esta misma pregunta me siguió molestando

durante un cierto tiempo, ya que ella acudía a trabajar con cojera y les contó a las secretarias que estaba durmiendo poco debido al dolor. Haber tenido éxito me produjo un placer indudable, pero, al mismo tiempo, no pude evitar sentirme culpable de su malestar.

Finalmente, después de un año viéndola sufrir, decidí que se había hecho justicia y que mi venganza era completa. Entonces, retiré los alfileres de la pierna de la muñeca con evidente satisfacción y los deseché. Al día siguiente, el cirujano que atendió a mi colega tuvo una inspiración. Consideró que el clavo ortopédico estaba relacionado con su dolor residual y decidió que era hora de quitarlo. Milagrosamente, mi colega está libre de dolor desde entonces.

Esto era prueba concluyente de una causa-efecto asociada al hecho de que yo eliminara los alfileres de la muñeca. Mejor aún, mi colega nunca sospechó de las actividades misteriosas tras la puerta contigua.

Un nuevo elemento de esta historia me preocupa cada vez más. Mi amigo Marcel me había advertido que las fuerzas oscuras del vudú pueden volverse contra un practicante poco entrenado en estas artes mágicas de Haití. Los poderes que uno había usado podrían regresar a veces con igual fuerza, para atormentar a quien los había liberado.

Ahora estamos en 2020, durante la pandemia, mucho tiempo después de mi jubilación del hospital.

Este año mi pierna izquierda alcanzó la etapa final de la osteoartritis y necesité un reemplazo total de rodilla. Paradójicamente, ahora llevo dos gruesos clavos quirúrgicos de titanio tanto en el fémur como en la tibia. He pasado todo el año en una lenta y dolorosa rehabilitación, preguntándome si las fuerzas que una vez liberé se habrán vuelto contra mi propia pierna. O si no, ¿habrá algún otro practicando las tenebrosas artes del vudú para desearme daño con una muñeca que ahora tiene mi nombre?

SAUNA

El yogui americano a quien yo llamaba "Naga Baba" entró desnudo y francamente agitado en el sauna del Club Atlético. Aunque nos alarmaba su delgadez, era musculoso, y a pesar de su ansiedad aún mostraba rastros de su brillante sonrisa. Sus ojos negros y penetrantes escaneaban el pequeño espacio buscando su audiencia familiar y receptiva, hasta que al fin se desató: —¡Casi atropello a un mapache en la avenida Boren! ¿Qué podía estar haciendo este animal en una jungla de concreto, en donde no se ve ni un árbol? Estaba esquivando autos, aterrorizado. ¡Y ahora yo me siento igual!

Me apresuré a pedirle explicaciones antes de que comenzara a meditar como de costumbre. Me sorprendía verlo tan conmovido.

—Yo me siento como él, agredido por todos lados. El desorden de la política...la tecnología desenfrenada... ¿A ustedes no les afectan esos excéntricos de la informática que están invadiendo Seattle? —, preguntó—, esperando un comentario de apoyo. —Los

"

que más me aterrorizan son esos imberbes desaliñados y con acné. Me los encuentro en los ascensores, de pantalón corto aunque esté helando afuera. ¿Y qué hacen?, diseñan los juegos electrónicos que dejarán estúpida a toda una generación—. Todavía ansioso por su encuentro con el mapache, terminó agregando, con un suspiro: —Por eso que este sauna es para mí un santuario. Aquí puedo practicar yoga, meditar, y cantar los mantras que me enseñaron—. Decía haber estudiado en un templo de la India por varios años, y estaba muy enfocado en sus objetivos: lograr el estado de *moksa* e interrumpir el eterno ciclo del nacer y renacer.

Terminado su discurso, comenzó a meditar y se desconectó del mundo por varios minutos. En el banco de enfrente, Gabriel —un lector empedernido, enfrascado en una novela latinoamericana—suspendió la lectura (cosa muy rara) y lo miró con curiosidad.

—Discúlpame, Arturo, quizás sea una ilusión óptica porque aquí está más oscuro que en un club nocturno tailandés. ¡Pero me parece ver una pulgada de espacio entre tus nalgas y el banco! ¿Te estás levitando?

En postura *padmasana*, las caderas relajadas y las piernas cruzadas en un ángulo muy pronunciado (la culminación de muchos años de práctica), Naga Baba miró al colombiano con una leve sonrisa y le respondió con aire pensativo:

—No, por qué los grandes yoguis creen que levitar es de fanfarrones, ya que no ayuda a obtener la liberación. Yo soy un yogui avanzado pero no soy un *sadhu.* Si uno de estos hombres santos alcanzara aquí el estado de *moksa,* su espíritu dejaría el cuerpo para unirse con la conciencia universal. Yo he tratado eso durante años, pero sin éxito. Hay muy pocos que lo logren.

—¡Por favor, Arturo, no se te ocurra hacernos eso!— Le dijo Gabriel, algo preocupado. —Nos encantaría que llegaras a la liberación, ¿pero te imaginas el susto al entrar al sauna por la mañana y encontrar aquí tu cuerpo vacío? Resecado por el calor... largando olor... por favor, trata de llegar a la *moksa* en otra parte, ¿ok?, como ser... en tu templo cuando vuelvas a la India.

Al escuchar este intercambio, me sentí privilegiado de pertenecer a este pequeño grupo. El sauna era un microcosmos de esta ciudad fascinante y tan diversa. Esta impresión aumentó con la entrada de mi viejo amigo Marcelo, un haitiano musculoso pero flexible, quien se puso de inmediato a hacer flexiones, a estirar brazos, piernas y la columna, en preparación para la clase de artes marciales, sin dejar de observar de reojo al yogui, que ya estaba sudando profusamente. Marcelo, un analista de sistemas, sabía sobre las prácticas mágicas y misteriosas de su tierra. Nos había explicado que los haitianos eran un setenta por ciento católicos, treinta por ciento protestantes, y cien por ciento vudús, ahora una religión aceptada en su país. Él también conocía las creencias del Naga Baba. Lo que me sorprendió fue la propuesta que le hizo al yogui:

—Arturo, ¿Te conté alguna vez que tengo una

receta de mi abuelo para una poción casera con ron haitiano y otros ingredientes secretos? Dice tener un poderoso efecto psicológico, y podría ser un catalizador para tu búsqueda del *moksha.* ¿Estarías dispuesto a probarla? — El Naga Baba aceptó la idea de inmediato.

—¡Excelente! —, dijo Marcelo. —¡Si te da resultado, lo celebraremos bebiendo todos un poco del brebaje!

—Quizá podrías usar vudú también, Marcelo, con esas muñequitas negras que venden en New Orleans, para clavarles alfileres—, le dije descaradamente.

—¡No te lo creo! ¿Qué puede saber un investigador médico jubilado sobre mi religión? —, me dijo Marcelo, un poco ofendido porque me había metido en su elemento.

Entonces Gabriel nuevamente dejó de leer para escuchar mejor la conversación. Él dice poder escuchar música, o una redifusión multimedia y al mismo tiempo leer un libro. También asegura poder dividir su mente en compartimientos como Napoleón, leer y escuchar al mismo tiempo, sin perderse una palabra.

—Pancho, ¿cómo es posible que alguien educado como tú sea tan supersticioso, y ande clavando alfileres en una muñequita? ¡Eso no coincide con la personalidad de uno que silba melodías de Mozart, o la Arlesiana de Bizet debajo de la ducha!

—Un momento, ¿por qué me llamaste 'Pancho'?

—Te hacía falta un sobrenombre, y ese te queda bien, después del que le pusiste a Arturo. Me haces acordar a Pancho Villa, otro latino corpulento y bravucón, con un bigote sin recortar. La única diferencia es que él no usaba anteojos oscuros de marca Zero-G. Desde ahora te voy a llamar Pancho.

La idea de Marcelo de preparar un brebaje mágico me impulsó a consultar a otros habitués del sauna sobre cómo ayudar al yogui (aunque él no lo había solicitado). Al primero que encontré fue a Gabriel leyendo bajo la ducha. Tenía la novela en la mano izquierda, con el brazo estirado para que no se mojara. Eso no me sorprendió, ya que lo había visto otras veces nadando en el club, y paraba cada pocos largos para leer de un libro que dejaba en el extremo de la piscina. Otra vez lo vimos en el sauna con una venda en su canilla derecha. Mientras caminaba hacia su casa por la noche, leyendo con una lámpara en la frente, tropezó contra una barra metálica para amarrar las bicicletas. Un psicoanalista amigo una vez me sugirió que le preguntara a Gabriel: —Si tuvieses que parar de leer, ¿te da miedo lo que podrías pensar?

Gabriel no tenía otras sugerencias prácticas, pero en cambio me dijo que se sentía un poco culpable de haber provocado al yogui. Me preguntó qué me parecía si le regalaba una vieja edición de 'Siddhartha', el libro de Herman Hesse que había sido un culto cuando Gabriel era un adolescente en Bogotá. Ese gesto me pareció muy loable.

Saliendo del club me encontré con Pratik, otro de los habituales de la sauna y un admirador incondicional del yogui. Él había nacido en la India y fue educado como un hindú, aunque decía no ser muy creyente. Igual tenía esperanzas de que Naga Baba, con su conocimiento profundo del hinduismo, lo pudiese ayudar a descifrar el significado real del "espacio del Dharma". También admiraba el lado humano del yogui, y su compromiso por el bienestar de la "vaca sagrada"; incluso habían ido juntos a visitar un tambo para observar los métodos de producción. Él apreciaba la actitud del Naga Baba de poner en contacto entre ellos a la gente que él más apreciaba—de hecho, había sido el yogui quién me había presentado a Pratik en la sauna.

Respecto a cómo ayudar al yogui en su desarrollo espiritual, Pratik prefería encontrar un método técnico para comprender la meditación profunda, aunque no era un experto en la materia. Su campo era el comercio electrónico en los países en desarrollo, y escribía una columna en el DailyO, un programa en la red con gran difusión internacional.

Más tarde, soñando despierto en mi café favorito, se me ocurrió cómo captar la imagen de la función cerebral del yogui durante su meditación profunda. Entonces llamé a mi amigo Max, un investigador del Instituto Allen de Neurociencia. A él le encantaba demostrar sus recientes éxitos en visualizar los circuitos nerviosos del cerebro humano. Max también jugaba al squash en el Club Atlético y frecuentaba el sauna, de modo que sabía de las prácticas y de la búsqueda espiritual del Naga Baba.

Apenas entré al laboratorio de Max me encontré frente a frente con algo parecido a un cerebro viviente que flotaba en el centro de la sala. La imagen tridimensional ilustraba una red impresionante de conexiones multicolores que, para mi ojo inexperto, se extendían en muchas direcciones como al azar. Mi amigo estaba usando los equipos más modernos de realidad virtual, y programas de inteligencia artificial para trazar mapas de la función cerebral profunda. Había logrado reducir el tamaño de sus instrumentos hasta caber en una cajita como la de un teléfono celular.

Yo fui derecho al grano: —Max, ¡tu método es fabuloso! ¿No podrías aplicarlo para visualizar el cerebro del Naga Baba durante su meditación profunda? Yo lo vengo observando por un tiempo, y creo que está por lograr su objetivo. ¿No podrías captarlo en el instante preciso en que se libere de esta vida material?

—¿En serio, Armando? De a ratos me parece que vos, Marcelo y Gabriel son unos charlatanes—. Sonaba dudoso, pero no rechazó del todo mi propuesta. —Esta tecnología podría ser la mejor que hay para explorar estas ideas. Pero tendríamos que estar allí cuando Arturo llegue al nivel más profundo para cacharlo con 'las manos en la masa'. ¿No podrías persuadirlo a participar como sujeto de pruebas? Él tendría que venir a mi laboratorio para una serie de grabaciones mientras está conectado durante la meditación—. Hizo una pequeña pausa, antes de concluir: —Entretanto, ¿podrías traerme unas fotos suyas meditando, tomadas desde muchos ángulos? Eso me ayudaría a crear un modelo para producir las imágenes.

No tuve problemas en convencer al yogui a participar en el experimento, quién vino fielmente por varias semanas a las sesiones de laboratorio. Apenas pude, aparecí en el vestuario del club cargado con mis cámaras Leica y con un trípode muy estable para fotografiarlo meditando sobre el banco de madera, mirando hacia su casillero favorito, el número 741. Como éramos asiduos en el club, nadie preguntó por la sesión fotográfica. Arturo ya estaba meditando, con la piel brillante por la aplicación de aceite de coco y de su crema Ayurvédica predilecta. Fue fácil encontrarlo luego de su sesión de yoga en el sauna, que él hacía regularmente dos veces por la mañana y dos al atardecer, por treinta minutos cada vez. Era un programa agotador que lo dejaba deshidratado y desesperado de sed, la que calmaba con dos vasos de agua de coco con limón muy fría, ya lista esperándolo en el vestuario. Se había desmayado un par de veces al pasar sus límites de treinta minutos, y una vez hubo que rescatarlo porque se había caído y golpeado la cabeza sobre el banco, y sangraba profusamente. Eso lo había avergonzado mucho. Yo comencé a fotografiarlo y pronto estaba tan inmóvil como la esfinge de Guiza, respirando apenas, y tan lentamente que no se podía asegurar que estaba vivo. Los socios quedaban estupefactos al ver a este flaquísimo personaje inmóvil, y algunos hasta paraban para observarlo por unos segundos, antes de irse sacudiendo la cabeza. Los que lo conocíamos mejor, en cambio nos preguntábamos si quizás no estaría por alcanzar su objetivo espiritual.

Más tarde en el laboratorio, Max se mostró satisfecho con las fotografías de alta resolución que le había llevado. Aun siendo un científico riguroso, tenía gran curiosidad y entusiasmo por mi fantasioso proyecto. Entonces me propuso que hagamos un ensayo en el club con las primeras imágenes digitales del cerebro del Naga Baba, pero un día en que él no estaría en el club. Max no quería influenciar la mente del yogui mostrándole su propia actividad cerebral tan temprano en el estudio. Nos pusimos de acuerdo en hacerlo pronto.

Pocos días más tarde me enteré de que Naga Baba saldría de vacaciones en Florida para visitar a sus hijos ya grandes, que iban a correr en una carrera. Igual que su padre, ambos eran maratonistas muy reputados. Cuando le dije a Max, me sugirió encontrarnos exactamente a las seis de la tarde, cuando el club estaba más frecuentado, para probar sus instrumentos en el vestuario. Entonces les pedimos a los socios que conocíamos mejor que viniesen a la hora justa, para una presentación visual de los circuitos neurales del cerebro del yogui.

Llegado el momento, algunos de nosotros nos dejamos llevar hacia el vestuario, sin saber muy bien lo que esperar. Para nuestra sorpresa, el casillero No. 741 estaba abierto por completo, con la consabida botella de aceite de coco bien visible en el interior. Supuestamente, el yogui había cambiado sus planes de asistir a la maratón en Florida, porque allí estaba, sentado en su clásica pose del Loto, mirando hacia el casillero y brillando de sudor después del sauna de la tarde y la sesión de yoga. Lo observamos en silencio por un par de minutos sin querer interrumpir su rutina, y nos asombró ver aparecer un espacio entre su cuerpo y el banco de madera. ¡El hueco parecía crecer hasta tener casi dos pulgadas de alto! ¿No estaría levitando a pesar de su oposición declarada a estas proezas?

De pronto, vimos una llama de color naranja rojizo, muy sutil, surgir de la cima de su cabeza y crecer hasta casi un pie de altura, al principio vibrando lentamente, y luego con mucha más fuerza, mientras cambiaba a un tono rojo intenso. El grupo entero estaba en shock y nadie comprendía lo que pasaba, mientras más gente se congregaba a nuestro alrededor en un silencio total, hasta que alguien llamó al gerente del club para que viniese a ver este fenómeno.

Entonces, el cuerpo del yogui comenzó a flotar, quizá como un pie más alto hacia el techo, dejando un espacio vacío debajo suyo. Inesperadamente, la llama roja se extinguió como si alguien hubiese apagado la luz de la sala. El cuerpo del yogui volvió a caer sobre el banco, como magnetizado por la Tierra misma, siempre en la pose del *padmasana*. Permaneció inmóvil por unos segundos y comenzó a esfumarse hasta desaparecer por completo, dejando solo un triste banco vacío. El único signo de su presencia reciente era el fuerte aroma del aceite de coco que conocíamos tan bien.

Un pandemonio estalló en el vestuario. Todos parecían de acuerdo en que finalmente Naga Baba había llegado a la liberación, y que lo había logrado nada menos que aquí en el Club, entre sus amigos. Estábamos pasmados de haber presenciado el momento preciso en que un yogui arribó a la *moksa*. Pero no quedaba claro cómo se había arreglado para no dejar su cuerpo detrás por más de unos pocos segundos, quizá para evitar que tuviéramos que deshacernos de sus restos mortales. Marcelo lagrimeaba en silencio, repitiendo por lo bajo algo que parecía ser su propio mantra: —El jarabe de ron de mi abuelo fue lo que lo ayudó. ¡Lo ayudó de verdad!

Todos salimos del vestuario en tropel y maravillados, especulando sin control sobre este suceso extraordinario. Pero pensando con tristeza que el yogui no había estado conectado a los instrumentos en el momento de su liberación. Ahora el mundo no llegaría a saber lo sucedido en su cerebro en ese momento crítico. Por otro lado, yo me felicité por la inspiración de pedirle a Max que sea nuestro experto científico. Quizás todavía podríamos aprender más con los datos obtenidos en las sesiones de meditación. Es posible que la poderosa energía mental colectiva de nuestros amigos había llegado a una masa crítica, para unirse a la del yogui en camino hacia su meta de liberación espiritual.

El Club Atlético entero, especialmente los habituales del sauna, estaban agitadísimos y cada uno tenía una teoría diferente sobre lo ocurrido. Alguien había llamado a los diarios, y la prensa estaba en camino para investigar. Las noticias del incidente podían potencialmente llegar a ser distribuidas sin límites en el internet, ya que nadie en Occidente había presenciado jamás el momento en que un yogui alcanzaba la *moksa*.

Cuando finalmente pude sentarme con Max, alejados de los otros socios, le pregunté por su opinión. Lo que había pasado era muy diferente de lo que yo esperaba. Yo venía interesado en ver su presentación científica, y una visión preliminar del cerebro del yogui como la que había admirado en su oficina, ¡pero en cambio me encontré con un milagro!

Max sacó del bolsillo una cajita como la que había visto en su laboratorio, un proyector en miniatura, y me la mostró con la expresión petulante de un alquimista que hubiera descubierto la piedra filosofal. Y allí me dijo:

—No hay que tomar al pie de la letra lo que hemos visto, Armando. A veces esperamos intensamente que pase algo y estamos dispuestos a aceptar que lo que vimos es una realidad. De hecho, yo estaba muy impresionado con la determinación del yogui, y con el apoyo apasionado de sus amigos, de modo que me dejé llevar por el entusiasmo. Y con al ánimo de satisfacer es posible que mis ideas me llevaran demasiado lejos. ¡Por eso que lo que vieron todos es solo un holograma basado en tus fotografías del yogui meditando! Las imágenes están basadas en antiguas crónicas de casos de *moksa* en la India.

—Espera un momento, Max. ¡Qué desilusión! Yo también soy científico, pero he buscado toda mi vida una prueba contundente de que se puede trascender esta vida material usando prácticas espirituales. Por eso me fascinó ver con mis propios ojos a un yogui llegar a la iluminación usando la meditación profunda. Al menos quisiera saber hasta dónde había avanzado él durante la última grabación—. Yo insistí, para saber si habíamos encontrado signos concretos de su progreso espiritual hacia la meta.

—Por favor, no te lo tomes tan a pecho. ¿No podrías guardar el secreto un ratito más? Yo confiaba en darles una idea de la belleza de cuando Naga Baba llegue a la iluminación. Pero en realidad, él nunca pudo profundizar su meditación por encima de lo que conseguía en el sauna. Cuando vuelva de su viaje vamos a continuar las sesiones, aunque me temo que pasará mucho tiempo hasta poder observar su mente en el instante preciso en que se una a la conciencia universal.

—Lo más difícil ahora va a ser como sobrevivir a la indignación de nuestros amigos y socios del club cuando les expliquemos, y pidamos disculpas por el teatro que presenciaron. Ojalá me perdonen por haberles mostrado una ilusión óptica tan optimista. Bueno, ahora mejor que nos escurramos en silencio antes de que llegue la prensa, para encontrar a Gabriel y Marcelo. Nos merecemos una recompensa por nuestro dramático éxito tecnológico. Vamos a probar el místico brebaje de ron, y quizás me dé coraje por decirles la verdad sobre lo que ha pasado.

Pudimos sobrevivir a la ira de los socios, pero no estábamos preparados para otra sorpresa. Después de mostrarles el holograma, nadie más volvió a ver al yogui. Estaba ausente en las sesiones de laboratorio, y del sauna, y el gerente dijo que Arturo había dejado de pagar las cuotas mensuales y que se retiró de la ciudad sin explicación. Pratik en especial estaba desilusionado "de que se hubiese escapado como un mafioso y partido sin honor". Él creía que el yogui era muy terco y orgulloso al no querer llevar al sauna su botella de agua, y sospechaba que "estaba avergonzado por los desmayos y las caídas en el sauna". Después agregó que estaba ofendido, porque —Arturo resultó ser muy distinto a lo que pretendía ser entre nosotros—. Incluso nos contó que —al salir a comer con amigos, hasta había probado carne de los platos de otros ya que era gratis, aunque afirmaba ser estrictamente vegetariano.

Unos meses más tarde, Pratik descubrió fotos del yogui en Facebook, que lo mostraban como un extra en un estudio de Hollywood. Lo que más lo angustiaba era que, —si bien el yogui pretendía seguir la vía del Dharma, en realidad no era más que un hippy obsesivo y sin remedio.

Finalmente, Pratik recibió un mensaje electrónico del Naga Baba:

"Pratik prabhu, mi estimado amigo, ciertamente por muchas encarnaciones pasadas: Por favor dígale a mi otro amigo Armando que el mapache que estaba acorralado y aterrorizado en medio de una avenida en Seattle se trasladó, pero sigue igualmente acorralado y aterrorizado en la jungla de la industria cinematográfica de Hollywood.

¡Amor y Paz para todos ustedes, mis queridos amigos de Seattle!"

NASTASSIA

Para Mariana:
Que nunca llegue a inspirarnos
con la "aburrición".

El día en que Nastassia Vanholder-Lacroix sufrió otra transformación espectacular, su marido decidió tomar cartas en el asunto. Entonces canceló la reunión con su agente de aduana —algo dramático y poco común— y, en cambio, se comunicó conmigo, un amigo de confianza y un psicoanalista conocido, para pedir ayuda. Cuando nos encontramos, Phil estaba sumergiendo nerviosamente un biscotto en el cappuccino caliente, y soltó de pronto:

—Maurice, ¿estás de acuerdo con que el realismo mágico ha muerto? ¡Ya no puede competir con la complejidad surreal de nuestras propias vidas!

Como de costumbre, esa primera frase no hacía referencia directa al extraño comportamiento de Nastassia; pero sí mostraba un concepto de la existencia humana en otra dimensión, o en un universo teórico. Aún ahora que conozco el caso, dudo si ese arrebato reflejaba la desaparición de ese estilo en la literatura latinoamericana, o su inquietud por los inexplicables cambios de apariencia y de conducta de su esposa.

—¡Por favor, quisiera que me ayudaras! Necesito tu experiencia de psicoanalista y tu conocimiento sobre ciertas doctrinas esotéricas del Oriente.

De repente dejó de jugar con el biscotto, intentó adoptar una postura más relajada pero abandonó enseguida ese objetivo.

Cuando quedamos, la condición de Nastassia ya había despertado la imaginación de nuestro grupo de gastrónomos empedernidos y adictos al café en Seattle. Nuestro reino celestial era la cavernosa sala, con muros de madera oscura, de la Torrefazione Toscana, un paraíso de la cafetería en medio de las eternas lluvias que caracterizan la región. Este centro magnético atraía a nuestra pequeña comunidad de exilados hipercríticos, convencidos de que allí servían un aromático espresso tostado a la perfección, con un sabor intenso, sin regusto desagradable y de que era el más italiano de la ciudad. Las bellas tacitas de cerámica, decoradas al estilo florentino, completaban la experiencia.

Aparte de la calidad del café, la Torrefazione era un microcosmo de eclécticos personajes que circulaban por su mostrador. Había arquitectos, galeristas, otros sin domicilio y necesitados de una buena taza de café caliente, informáticos que trabajaban en el barrio y algún literato en busca de un lugar estimulante para la creación de sus ficciones. En general, el establecimiento era muy pacífico, pero algo inesperado, como el caso de Nastassia Vanholder-Lacroix, podía sembrar el caos. Todo comenzó con su teatral llegada al puerto de Seattle y su recepción por un grupo numeroso de nuestros amigos del café. Asombrados, la vimos bajar la rampa del buque de carga holandés como una modelo profesional y, al mismo tiempo, con elegancia natural. El espectáculo llenaba a mi amigo Phil de orgullo y admiración.

Philip, Phil Good y Nastassia se habían casado en los Países Bajos, en una desbordante ceremonia sobre una barcaza de río, anclada en el canal Heerrengracht, en Ámsterdam. Ella era una conocida diseñadora de alta costura, tan a gusto en los grandes bulevares de París o en el centro de Londres como en las boutiques de Milán. Delgada y oscura, de una belleza excéntrica, modelaba sus propias creaciones durante semanas antes de presentarlas a la prensa. A diferencia de otros diseñadores, su gusto impecable se complementaba con una preparación técnica rigurosa en la famosa École des Beaux Arts de París y el Instituto Tecnológico de Praga. Tenía preferencia por unos textiles exquisitos para crear atuendos tipo kimono, inspirados en la tradición samurái del Japón medieval. Al vestirse con estos conjuntos casi militares de color gris o índigo, podía presentarse despreocupada tanto en un supermercado estadounidense como en una fiesta elegante en París, las que organizaba con frecuencia en el Marais.

Phil me había hablado de su primer encuentro casual con ella, durante uno de sus viajes a Nepal. Él buscaba antiguos manuscritos tibetanos para "importarlos", de algún modo dudoso, a los Estados Unidos. Los dos se habían cruzado en un camino nevado a casi 4.000 metros de altura. La aparición de una mujer delgada con un kimono, que hablaba con acento holandés, con modales europeos y dejaba un rastro de perfume francés, le hizo perder la respiración. Se casaron pocos meses más tarde y ahora Nastassia venía camino a Seattle, en donde nuestra estirada comunidad cafetera la recibió con los brazos abiertos. Su relación con Phil se fortaleció con el tiempo. Por otra parte, la comunidad los consideraba una pareja ideal, aventurera y atractiva, y les auguraba un maravilloso futuro juntos.

Poco después de su llegada, comenzamos a estrechar relaciones, y una noche los invité a cenar en casa. A pedido de Nastassia, les ofrecí una cacerola de pescado aromático, receta que había adaptado de Roy Andries de Groot, un admirado chef nacido en Inglaterra, pero de profundas raíces holandesas. En este caso me tomé ciertas libertades con la receta. El mismo De Groot había declarado: "El maridaje perfecto de comida y vino debería permitir las infidelidades".

Durante la cena, Nastassia me preguntó:

—Maurice, ¿no pondrías alguna música apropiada para esta comida tan deliciosa?

Me dirigí hacia el tocadiscos y elegí una sonata para piano de Mozart, tocada por Lily Kraus, una renombrada intérprete de Mozart y de Beethoven. Confiado en que ella apreciaría la pieza, no estaba preparado para su sorpresiva reacción. En cuanto escuchó las primeras notas de la sonata, se lanzó a sollozar ruidosamente, lagrimeando desconsolada mientras se cubría el rostro con las manos. Apagué la música de inmediato y volví a la mesa para averiguar qué le pasaba.

—No te alarmes, Maurice —dijo Phil para calmar las cosas—. Nastassia es sumamente sensible a la música de Mozart. Le encanta, pero al mismo tiempo le trae recuerdos y una intensa pena.

Nastassia se recuperó al rato y se disculpó:

—Perdona por el numerito, Maurice. Admiro mucho a Mozart, pero es demasiado para mí. Su música me produce una profunda tristeza. Por favor, pon algo más, cualquier otra cosa.

Debería haberme dado cuenta de que la hipersensibilidad de Nastassia era un indicio de otros episodios futuros. Ninguno de los que frecuentábamos el café había imaginado a su llegada que sólo unos meses más tarde nos veríamos en acaloradas discusiones sobre las causas y las implicaciones del comportamiento de Nastassia. Ese cambio repentino y extravagante fue lo que llevó a Phil a solicitar mi ayuda.

* * *

Varios días después de que me llamara, nos encontramos de nuevo para hablar de la situación con un café. Lo primero que dijo Phil fue:

—¿Te acuerdas de Zelig, el personaje de Woody Allen que se transmuta como un camaleón? Él podía adoptar la apariencia externa, la psicología y el comportamiento de la gente que lo rodeaba. Creo que Nastassia está afectada por un síndrome similar. No se me ocurre otra explicación racional.

—¿Has hablado con ella? ¿Es consciente de sus transformaciones y de la reacción que causan en otras personas?

—Al principio, negaba las preocupaciones de todos y atribuía los cambios a la originalidad de su propio estilo. Con su acento inimitable y su peculiar fraseo en inglés, me contó que era la respuesta a la "aburrición" de su nueva vida en Estados Unidos. Tal vez este fastidio sea la causa de estos raros incidentes.

Consideré varios diagnósticos psiquiátricos, sin decidirme por ninguno, ya que las tales "transformaciones" no eran síntomas concluyentes.

—Sufrió un primer episodio durante una reciente visita a Londres —prosiguió Phil—. Mientras explorábamos South Kensington, nos topamos con un restaurante tradicional indio, el Kerala Spice Trail, donde disfrutamos de una deliciosa y romántica comida. Terminamos con fruta fresca recién llegada de la India. Ella describió el postre como el mejor mango que jamás había probado, pero luego se quedó extrañamente callada. Después del almuerzo, nos separamos por unas horas. Yo fui a ver a un comerciante de antigüedades chino, quien intentaba venderme un buda camboyano. Supuestamente, André Malraux lo introdujo de contrabando en uno de sus primeros viajes a Angkor. Mientras tanto, Nastassia fue a pasear por su cuenta, sin ningún destino en mente. Ambos regresamos al hotel a las ocho de la tarde y entramos por la puerta giratoria al mismo tiempo, en dirección hacia el ascensor. ¿Puedes creer que al principio no la reconocí? Estaba vestida con un colorido sari, tenía un circulito púrpura pintado en la frente y exudaba un curioso aroma a cardamomo y comino. Lo más inexplicable fue que ella no hablaba con su acento habitual de amsterdamer, ¡pero pronunciaba el inglés como una persona de Kerala!

—¿Su apariencia y comportamiento fueron algo temporal o se convirtieron en rasgos permanentes?

—Esta fase o, debería decir, fenómeno, duró varios días. Nastassia parecía normal, pero había adoptado la apariencia, el estilo y la psicología de una elegante mujer india.

Phil reflexionó por un momento, antes de continuar:

—Quizá recuerdes que, cuando regresamos a los Estados Unidos, ella estuvo así durante un tiempo, lo cual despertó la curiosidad de todos. Al principio, atribuimos este comportamiento a su excentricidad, pero pronto quedó claro que estábamos equivocados porque se transformó de nuevo, esta vez en...

—¡Espera, Phil! ¿Hubo algo que pudiera haberle facilitado ese cambio?

—Tal vez tengas razón. Una tarde nos encontramos con una amiga, una culturista y corredora de maratones, ya sabés, como los que se ven en Seattle, en especial cerca de la universidad o en la orilla del lago. Ella le ofreció a Nastassia un bocado de su power bar, aparentemente su almuerzo diario, con nueces y bayas, y compartieron un trago de su power jock juice, una bebida para atletas. La noche siguiente Nastassia estaba en casa vestida con pantalones de licra azul eléctrico y una camiseta, y lucía un peinado corto y masculino. El perfume indio, el acento de Kerala y el sari habían desaparecido, y ella me saludó con una expresión que nunca había usado antes: "¡Choca los cinco!", con un acento muy americano. Curiosamente, unos días después pareció volverse más musculosa y adquirió una tremenda resistencia física. De hecho, participó en una carrera de diez kilómetros y terminó junto a los corredores más rápidos, aunque nunca se había entrenado antes. Debo confesar que no me gustaron ni su nueva apariencia ni sus impropios modales, casi vulgares.

—Por supuesto, estos cambios son asombrosos, pero hasta ahora no veo una explicación clara.

Yo me preguntaba, en mi interior, si ella habría participado en un ritual religioso o tántrico o en sesiones de meditación profunda, ya que algunos sostienen que pueden revivir recuerdos de encarnaciones previas. La verdad es que no sabía cómo ayudarlos. Necesitaba más información, que Phil podía conocer.

—¿Estaba tomando drogas?

—Nada en absoluto. Pero otros factores desencadenantes parecen provocar esos cambios con rapidez. Como cuando celebramos el cumpleaños de un amigo en Shanghái Gate, un buen restaurante chino en el Distrito Internacional. Los frijoles con camarones importados de China y la variedad de hongos eran excepcionales. Debido a que esa noche tuve sueños muy vívidos, me pregunté si un hongo psicodélico podría haber contaminado la maravillosa cena. Como era de esperar, al otro día, por la tarde, Nastassia había adoptado la apariencia regia de una viuda mandarina o de madama en un burdel de Shanghái antes de la guerra. Su cabello, normalmente oscuro, se había vuelto negro, mientras que sus ojos se habían achinado. Una larga y fluida túnica de seda china la envolvía como si hubiera nacido con ella puesta.

Phil estaba obviamente trastornado. Ahora evitaba a los conocidos; había dejado de jugar al squash, su deporte favorito, y no se lo divisaba por las galerías de arte, en donde solía rastrear antigüedades asiáticas o manuscritos olvidados.

—Sus transformaciones se han vuelto intolerables para los dos. Ella quisiera acabar con estos cambios que no me gustan, y ahora le preocupa que la gente la esté evitando, mirando con recelo o apartándose abiertamente cuando llega, como temiendo lo que ella pudiera llegar a hacer. ¡Ojalá puedas ayudarnos!

Sin duda estaba bastante angustiado, dejaba caer su biscotto, lo recogía y enseguida lo descartaba con una mirada superficial. Lo vi añadir más azúcar a su cappuccino y poner mala cara, como si la dulzura le resultara intolerable. Finalmente continuó describiendo, a tropezones, el último giro de los acontecimientos:

—Hace poco viajamos a Muskogee, Oklahoma, para visitar a unos parientes lejanos. Como sabrás, no estoy muy entusiasmado por esta rama muy conservadora de mi familia. Llegamos justo para el famoso Festival de la Serpiente de Cascabel. Lo más fascinante fue ver la destreza del carnicero del pueblo. Cazadores de todas las edades le traían sus víboras para competir, ya que daban premios a la más grande, a la más pequeña y a la más venenosa. Como todo el mundo, probamos un sándwich de serpiente, que no es muy diferente a uno de pollo o conejo. Como me temí, sin comunicarlo a mis amigos, en parte por vergüenza, desde ese día Nastassia ha estado usando vaqueros, lo que nunca hizo en el pasado, los Lee, para precisar; una camisa de cuadros y botas de piel de lagarto. Una misteriosa cola de caballo rubia ha reemplazado su peinado de emperatriz viuda. Ahora la música estridente de Woody Guthrie nos sacude la casa, ¡y ella está tomando sémola de maíz en el desayuno, por el amor de Dios! También encontré un paquete sospechoso en nuestro congelador, con trozos alargados de carne blanca... y puedo adivinar de dónde viene —concluyó.

Me alarmé cuando comenzó a sudar y al ver sus pupilas dilatadas, como a punto de sufrir un ataque de pánico.

—Tranquilo, Phil. Haré lo que esté en mis manos para ayudarlos. Por supuesto, podría intentar la hipnosis, si ella me lo permitiera. Eso es lo que hizo Mia Farrow, la psiquiatra de Woody en la película que mencionaste antes. Pero estoy desarrollando una teoría razonable, menos esotérica de lo que buscabas. Idealmente, me gustaría entrevistar a Nastassia en persona, pero sospecho que ella podría no estar de acuerdo.

Reflexioné sobre el caso, antes de proseguir:

—Su desconcertante metamorfosis me hizo pensar en los escritos de G. K. Chesterton, famoso por la serie del Padre Brown, detective. ¿Has leído sus misterios cristianos o El hombre que sabía demasiado? Según él, suele haber una explicación racional a algo en apariencia inexplicable o sobrenatural. Según este razonamiento, podríamos estar frente a una paradoja, en lugar de un milagro. Si aceptamos que este misterio puede haber ocurrido en cualquiera de los múltiples universos o dimensiones, se deduce que también debería haber infinitas soluciones, una de las cuales podría explicar los hechos en su totalidad.

Yo era consciente de mi tono pseudocientífico, pero no dejé de sentirme importante. De alguna manera, tenía que ser útil, definir un enfoque práctico, más razonable y realista.

Phil parecía haberse animado en cierto modo con mi explicación. Continué:

—Creo que la causa desencadenante de estos cambios es un estímulo gustativo, posiblemente la ingesta de ciertos alimentos que podrían despertar su inagotable memoria del gusto. Por ejemplo, ese delicioso mango en el restaurante Kerala debe haber provocado un poderoso recuerdo, que resurgió como un arquetipo genético en la forma de una mujer india por excelencia. El mango debe haberla transportado al espacio-tiempo en el que uno de sus antepasados, los Vanholder-Lacroix, tal vez comerciantes de la infame Compañía Holandesa de las Indias Orientales, pudo haberse acoplado con una belleza de Kerala, con profundos efectos impredecibles en generaciones futuras.

—¡Me gusta esta idea! Pero soy escéptico por naturaleza. Asumiendo que tu teoría sea correcta,

¿podrías sugerir un antídoto y hacer que vuelva a ser la diseñadora holandesa de antes? —Phil había dejado de probar la espuma de su taza y me observaba con atención, confiado en que daría una solución a los problemas de su esposa. Mi reputación infalible para los diagnósticos estaba en juego. Aun así, me arriesgué a profundizar, quizá cavando mi propia fosa:

—El tratamiento que propongo es la creación de fuertes asociaciones para revivir su experiencia de haber crecido en los Países Bajos. Para conseguir los productos indispensables, vas a requerir mucho ingenio y el uso de todos tus contactos. Deberías obtener, tan pronto como sea posible, por medios legales o no, ciertos alimentos que pueden ser difíciles de encontrar en Seattle —propuse. Aún no estaba seguro de estar en el camino correcto.

—¡No te preocupes, puedo hacerlo! Le preguntaré a Nastassia sobre lo que comía de niña. También voy a llamar a su madre, que está en Ámsterdam, para saber lo que a Nastassia le gustaba comer cuando era muy joven, pues quizá no lo recuerde.

—¡Esa es la actitud, Phil! La clave será identificar estos artículos y dárselos en pequeñas cantidades, a intervalos regulares, sobre todo, antes y después de sus incursiones en restaurantes étnicos, en especial cuando viaje al extranjero. Este programa es análogo a llevar un kit de mordedura de serpiente, o una jeringa de emergencia con epinefrina para gente alérgica a estos venenos —aseguré, con más confianza de lo que resultaba prudente en un caso tan inuisual.

Durante las semanas siguientes me sentía inquieto, a la espera de noticias de mis amigos. Llamé a Phil de vez en cuando por teléfono para interesarme por el progreso de Nastassia, pero parecía reticente a darme cualquier información. Finalmente, quedamos de nuevo en nuestro habitual café, la Torrefazione Toscana.

—¡Maurice, te estoy muy agradecido! Fue una gran idea consultarte sobre las misteriosas transformaciones de Nastassia. ¿Puedes creer que está respondiendo como tu pensaste? Se ha convertido de nuevo en la oscura diseñadora holandesa, de buen gusto, de la que me había enamorado a primera vista en el Himalaya.

—¿Cómo lograste estos excelentes resultados?

—Primero hablamos mucho sobre la infancia de Nastassia en Holanda. Entonces, le envié a su madre varios correos electrónicos para preguntarle si recordaba lo que su hija comía en ese entonces. De alguna manera, desarrollé un plan táctico para antagonizar lo que tú llamaste "metamorfosis desencadenada" por la memoria del gusto. Mi primera idea fue mantener un suministro permanente de varios quesos holandeses, como el Overjarige Boeren Kaas, que Nastassia ama y del que no puede prescindir. Entonces recurrí a mis contactos como importador de arte para encontrar un excelente proveedor de arenque y anguila ahumada, que Nastassia asociaría con su estadía en los balnearios del mar del Norte o su casa de verano en Volendam. Por si acaso, añadimos un poco de queso Edam, común del mismo distrito, aunque esto puede haber sido menos eficaz que el queso añejo y picante que mencioné antes.

—¿Se te ocurrieron otros alimentos que le evocaran recuerdos de cuando era joven?

—Sí. Pensé en algo muy efectivo. ¿Oíste hablar del Advokaat, esa bebida alcohólica dulce a base de huevo? A menudo sirve para aplacar a los niños pequeños en los Países Bajos. Se lo di al principio de su rehabilitación, cuando creí que podría ser más eficaz. Ahora guardamos varias muestras en el botiquín y en nuestros dos coches, y planeo darle una dosis completa al mínimo indicio de un ataque gustatorio. Finalmente, se me ocurrió algo que tu no habías sugerido. En un golpe de imaginación, o quizá de intuición, añadí un símbolo visual a su alrededor, que fue beneficioso para ambos. Te puedo decir, en confianza, que pude obtener una rara pintura de Vermeer (tal vez falsificada) de una hermosa joven desnuda y con solo un collar de perlas que, entre paréntesis, Nastassia ha encontrado curiosamente erótica y estimulante...

Su descripción era convincente y me contagió su entusiasmo. Me pregunté a mí mismo si habría pruebas concluyentes sobre los efectos de nuestra intervención. El resto de su relato lo confirmó con creces:

—La evidencia más sólida de su completa recuperación es que Nastassia viajó por su cuenta a Camboya, con la intención de comprar seda para sus diseños. En Phnom Penh oyó hablar de un pueblo de fabricantes de seda y contrató a un jovencito con una motocicleta para que la llevara, arriesgando la vida en las peligrosas carreteras rurales infestadas de minas. Allí conoció a un notable grupo de mujeres que tejían seda maravillosa en patrones clásicos e intrincados, pero carecían de los medios para venderla. Nastassia ha implementado un sistema de microcréditos para ayudar a la aldea a expandir su negocio. Ella espera que las mujeres puedan producir seda en un volumen mucho mayor, vendérsela a un costo rentable, pero competitivo, y tal vez incluso quieran aprender con ella técnicas de alta costura para asistir en la confección de sus diseños.

Phil y Nastassia han regresado a nuestro grupo en la Torrefazione y, nuevamente, hay calma en las reuniones, ahora que estamos seguros de su salud mental. Ella parece tan elegante y jubilosa como siempre, se ha adaptado a su vida aquí y ya no se queja de "aburrición" en Estados Unidos. Por mi parte, me siento muy recompensado por su clara mejoría. Como un beneficio inesperado, ahora recibo consultas sobre otras situaciones inusuales de diferentes miembros de nuestra comunidad cafetera.

Concebido en la noche de Año Nuevo de 1993. Revisado durante la pandemia del año 2020, como un proyecto de supervivencia.

EL HOMBRE QUE APRENDIÓ A AMAR LA BOMBA

El señor G. entró despacito al consultorio, con timidez o desconfianza. Vestía un saco de tweed marrón, algo raído, camisa blanca sin planchar y una corbata de rayas de algún regimiento inglés; imaginé que podría ser profesor de colegio secundario. Se presentó con poca energía, se sentó frente a mí y me explicó que tenía la presión arterial elevada. Su médico general le había recomendado consultar con un especialista porque el tratamiento previo no había sido eficaz. Pensé: "Esto parece un caso de rutina, en una persona poco interesante". Pero, como es frecuente en mi primera impresión, estaba doblemente equivocado.

Me dijo que era viudo, jubilado y que estaba un poco aburrido. En comparación con su vida anterior, ahora no encontraba suficiente motivación para seguir activo. Además, hacía un par de meses que le molestaban unos dolorcitos abdominales.

Lo revisé con cuidado, y creí palpar un pulso expansivo, bien profundo, por detrás del ombligo.

—Señor G., ¿cuál era su profesión?

—Soy veterano del ejército y experto en demoliciones. Durante la guerra de Corea me movilizaron para prestar mis servicios en sabotajes contra las tropas del norte. Me tocó destruir puentes sobre los ríos Yalu y Han, para dificultar las incursiones enemigas hacia Corea del Sur. Tuve suerte de no resultar herido ni tener accidentes, y me acostumbré de a poco al riesgo. Luego del ejército, por muchos años apliqué mi experiencia en trabajos civiles de construcción y en minas y canteras, hasta mi reciente jubilación. Y desde entonces estoy desanimado, sin interés por las cosas, duermo poco y mal.

—Lo siento. Me gustaría ayudarlo. Quisiera controlarle la presión y evaluar ese dolor que mencionó en el abdomen. Primero hablemos de su alimentación: le sugiero una dieta llamada "DASH", que consiste en comidas frescas, especialmente frutas y verduras, sin productos procesados ni en latas. Debo cambiarle un poco la medicación y voy a ordenar una ecografía abdominal. Es un estudio no invasivo y nada molesto.

Se despidió algo más alegre y prometió ocuparse un poco de sí mismo.

Cuando volvió por la clínica tres semanas más tarde, su presión había bajado hasta cerca de lo normal. Se lo veía menos cabizbajo y vestido igual, pero sin corbata. Quería saber el resultado de los estudios.

—Lo encuentro mejor, señor G., pero tuvimos una sorpresa en la ecografía: descubrimos un segmento de la aorta abdominal algo dilatado, lo que llamamos un aneurisma. Solo tiene tres o cuatro centímetros de diámetro, no es algo grave, pero podría ser la causa de sus dolores. Tendremos que repetir los exámenes con regularidad cada seis meses y fijarnos en su evolución. Además habría que agregar una medicina, un betabloqueante, para disminuir el impacto del pulso sobre el aneurisma. Este remedio a veces debilita un poco, pero nada más. Le recomendaría reducir algo sus actividades físicas, por ejemplo, no correr o saltar, para minimizar el riesgo.

A medida que le explicaba estos detalles, se mostraba más inquieto, balanceaba una pierna sobre la rodilla opuesta y le temblaban un poco las manos.

—Dígame, doctor, ¿cuál es el peligro de este aneurisma?

—Por favor, no se alarme, por ahora sólo debemos observarlo. Muchos son estables y no presentan complicaciones, pero si aumentara de diámetro con rapidez, sería preocupante. En ese caso, hay una posibilidad de ruptura espontánea. Creo que con el tratamiento vamos a controlarlo bien y observaremos su evolución.

—¿Se da cuenta, doctor, de que yo, un experto en explosivos, ahora tengo una bomba en mi propio cuerpo? Me va a resultar difícil adaptarme a esto. ¡Nunca tuve miedo a las bombas, pero esta la traigo puesta! Por un lado, usted me sugiere cuidarme más y evitar emociones y actividades de riesgo; pero por el otro, debería vivir más intensamente, aprovechar cada momento. Tendré que aprender a manejar las dos posibilidades.

Al retirarse, se movió algo inseguro hacia la puerta; estaba tan ensimismado que se olvidó de saludar o de mirar hacia atrás.

Al poco tiempo su presión estaba controlada y había perdido unas libras de peso. Sin embargo, el diámetro del aneurisma seguía aumentando hasta unos cinco centímetros de diámetro. Era consciente de que el señor G. luchaba contra un dilema, con dos situaciones contradictorias. Esto me obligó a renovar mis advertencias y a recomendar una vida tranquila y sin excitaciones. Me pregunté cómo iba a lograr un equilibrio entre dos opciones tan opuestas.

Luego de enterarse del crecimiento inexorable del aneurisma, el señor G. manifestó una transformación progresiva en su apariencia y su personalidad; esta era tan evidente como el deshielo de los glaciares en Groenlandia. Había cambiado su saco de tweed de profesor aburguesado por una campera de cuero tipo aviador, sobre una camisa de cuadros de colores y unos blue jeans que me parecieron ajustados para su edad. Pateaba casi desafiante unas botas de cuero de yacaré, insólitas en los Estados Unidos. Los ojos le brillaban con más intensidad de lo que recordaba en su primera visita, mientras me miraba satisfecho de sí mismo.

—Doctor —me dijo, inesperadamente—, ¿ha estado mirando las noticias en televisión? Ya debe saber mis novedades, como todo el mundo. Fue un verdadero espectáculo y me siento orgulloso del resultado. No hubo ningún herido y las casas de alrededor quedaron intactas.

—Perdone, señor G., pero no sé a qué se refiere. Lo veo muy entusiasmado. Cuénteme de qué se trata.

—¡De la demolición del Kingdome, el enorme estadio de béisbol con capacidad para 80.000 personas! Ha sido mi trabajo más importante desde el final de la guerra. Mi antiguo jefe me hizo llamar para dirigir la operación. Había que producir una implosión, con explosivos en sitios estratégicos para evitar daños en el vecindario y proteger los edificios y barracas de los alrededores.

—¡Lo felicito por el éxito de la ejecución! Fue impresionante. La había visto en las noticias, pero ni se me ocurrió que usted fuese el responsable. Pero ahora me preocupa que tenga un trabajo tan activo; ciertamente no es muy prudente para alguien con un aneurisma en crecimiento.

—El trabajo más duro lo hicieron mis ayudantes. Pero igual, fue una gran experiencia personal y, en cierto modo, me ha devuelto a la vida. Ahora duermo mejor y me despierto satisfecho. El ocio me afectaba muy negativamente. Estos cambios en mis actividades y recuperar mi autoestima me parecen más importantes que el riesgo del aneurisma. Estoy acostumbrado a las bombas y explosiones, pero el vacío interior me resultaba intolerable.

Pasaron unas pocas semanas, y una mañana recibí una llamada de uno de sus familiares:

—Doctor, le habla Laura, la hija del señor G. Necesito contarle que mi padre ha cambiado muchísimo desde que le diagnosticaron lo que él llama "mi bomba interior". Se ha vuelto muy irresponsable y no cumple con su tratamiento. Cada día comete más imprudencias y nos tiene alarmados. Lo llamo porque nos sorprendió con una nueva locura: se ha incorporado a un club de paracaidismo, algo que nunca había hecho. Dice que está entrenando para su primer salto de gran altura en los próximos días. ¡A su edad y con un aneurisma!

Por supuesto que intenté comunicarme con él, pero no respondió a mis llamados. El señor G. era un adulto y tendría que atenerse a las consecuencias.

Debió sobrevivir al salto, ya que se presentó en radiología para la ecografía prevista. Lamentablemente, el estudio demostró un aumento del diámetro de la lesión superior a los seis centímetros, un nivel crítico, de modo que le di cita para poco tiempo después.

—¿Cómo está, doctor? Lamento que mi hija lo haya molestado. Pero ya lo ve, no me ha pasado nada. Hice mi primer salto de gran altura y no hubo ninguna consecuencia, excepto para mi salud mental, que sigue mejorando cada día. La aventura fue extraordinaria, una experiencia que siempre había querido tener. Pero no se preocupe, mi presión arterial está controlada y no tengo efectos secundarios de los bloqueantes beta, como usted temía.

—¡Qué bueno, señor G.! Realmente, admiro su decisión de saltar en paracaídas, yo no me animaría hacerlo. Y me alegra el efecto positivo de su hazaña. Pero ahora lamento comunicarle, porque es mi obligación, que el aneurisma ha crecido rápidamente a más de seis centímetros. Eso aumenta el riesgo de ruptura, que podría ser catastrófica, y es una indicación para cirugía. Le sugiero iniciar una consulta con los cirujanos vasculares.

Lo pensó por un largo momento, antes de responderme:

—Doctor, prefiero no ver a los cirujanos. He leído un poco y hablado con gente amiga. Esa operación es muy difícil y me han dicho que tiene una mortalidad elevada. Ya estoy acostumbrado a llevar mi bomba puesta, porque es mi profesión, y la manejo con cuidado y con muchos años de experiencia. Prefiero dejarlo así y, a cambio, gozar de la vida como no lo había hecho por mucho tiempo. Se imagina, ¡el servicio técnico del ejército me ha pedido que vuelva a dar cursos de demolición a los nuevos cadetes, y también ayudar en algunos proyectos especializados! Es un riesgo bien calculado. Ya ve que mi presión está controlada. Considero que es mejor no hablar de cirugía por el momento. ¿No podríamos continuar con estas visitas, repitiendo la ecografía como hasta ahora?

—En estos casos, la decisión del paciente es muy importante. Entretanto, dígame, ¿cómo siguen sus dolores abdominales?

—Por suerte algo mejor, depende de lo que haya comido.

—Ese malestar podría también tener otras causas. ¿No me permite ordenar unos estudios más y una consulta con gastroenterología?

—Disculpe, doctor, ya estoy bastante preocupado con el aneurisma. Ya veremos más adelante si los dolores me siguen molestando. Voy a estar muy ocupado enseñando, y también me ofrecieron un trabajito en unas minas en Idaho, que aún no he aceptado. Si salgo de viaje y no puedo llamarlo, mi hija Laura podría comunicarse con usted. Además, ella también es geóloga y conoce a la perfección los métodos que usamos en minería. Ella podría tenerlo informado sobre mi salud y contarle mis actividades.

Aunque en estos tiempos los médicos estamos agobiados con tareas de administración, las recepcionistas y las enfermeras nos protegen para no recibir llamadas de afuera. Pero el caso del señor G. me preocupaba y asombraba al mismo tiempo. Por eso di órdenes de que no bloquearan las llamadas de Laura, para conocer las andanzas de mi peculiar paciente. Pronto me enteré de que se había cansado de enseñar a jóvenes cadetes en un cuartel y prefirió aceptar trabajos más expuestos y arriesgados, pero también interesantes. Primero participó en la demolición de grandes edificios antiguos, que serían reemplazados por masas de concreto y vidrio para alojar a técnicos recién llegados con el crecimiento de la informática. Luego aceptó una comisión de la marina militar para estudiar el efecto nocivo de explosiones submarinas en Puget Sound sobre las ballenas de la zona. Pero pronto Laura y yo perdimos contacto con él, cuando canceló el alquiler de su departamento en el centro para mudarse a Coeur D'Alene, en Idaho.

Traté de imaginar las razones de ese cambio drástico de domicilio. En esa región, conocida por la presencia de grupos de extrema derecha militante, armados y provocadores, se ubicaban las más grandes minas de plata del país; estas habían estado cerradas por varios años debido a la caída del precio de ese metal, pero leí que una de ellas iba a recomenzar la producción. Acto seguido, supuse que el señor G. no debía andar muy lejos de esa mina, ya que un experto en demoliciones sería esencial.

La siguiente llamada de Laura confirmó mis sospechas y aumentó mi ansiedad por este paciente tan insólito.

—Doctor, le agradezco mucho que reciba mis llamadas. Mi padre ha aceptado trabajar en la mina de plata, una operación con riesgos para todos, pero en especial para alguien con un aneurisma. Requiere un esfuerzo físico, aunque contará con suficientes ayudantes. La explosión suele ser bien controlada, pero los preparativos también conllevan peligro.

—¿Usan dinamita? —pregunté inocentemente.

—Hoy en día, para excavaciones profundas recurren al ANFO, una mezcla de 94,5 % de nitrato de amonio con un 5,5 % de gasolina diésel. Estas sustancias vienen por separado en camiones, las mezclan a último momento, y los gránulos son inyectados con aire comprimido en los tubos preinstalados. Esta misma mezcla se utiliza para prevenir las avalanchas en zonas muy nevadas.

—¿Cuál sería la diferencia con el fertilizante de nitrato de amonio? He leído que a veces explota espontáneamente, o en atentados terroristas.

—Esta sustancia, aun sin mezclar, puede deteriorarse con el tiempo y detonar por sí misma, aunque eso es bastante raro. Por suerte, el ANFO es un explosivo terciario, y precisa un detonador más otro promotor en cadena para que explote. Antes se recurría a la dinamita, pero hoy en día usan Tovex o pentolita. El drama es que los terroristas han aprendido estas combinaciones y en Oklahoma, en 1995, emplearon una combinación con nitrometano llamada ANNM.

—Bueno, Laura, si ya estaba preocupado por su padre antes de que hablásemos, ahora ya me siento aún más ansioso. Entiendo que él sea un experto, pero en su caso particular, creo que los riesgos son bastantes serios. Por favor, sigamos en contacto y cuénteme las novedades apenas las tenga.

Unos días más tarde, una noticia en el diario local me saltó a la vista: "Peligrosa explosión canceló la reapertura de una mina en Idaho". Había habido varios heridos, algunos graves, pero no mencionaban sus nombres. Muy inquieto, solicité a nuestra secretaria que buscara a Laura para informarme sobre su padre, pero nos fue imposible localizarla durante varios días. Hasta que una mañana ella me llamó al consultorio:

—Perdóneme, doctor, por no responder antes a su llamado, pero estaba acompañando a mi padre en Idaho. Lamento ser la emisaria de una triste noticia, él acaba de fallecer en el hospital de Coeur D'Alene.

—¡Cuánto lo siento! Estaba preocupado por él desde que supe del accidente en la mina de plata, ya que el diario no mencionaba el nombre de las víctimas.

—¡No me lo va a creer! Estaba bastante mal ya antes de la explosión en la mina, en la cual no llegó a participar. Pero mi padre falleció por complicaciones de un cáncer de colon. Él mismo no supo su diagnóstico hasta el último momento, antes de quedar inconsciente por un coma hepático. Pero podría asegurarle que en ningún momento se dejó desanimar por el aneurisma, y eso le ayudó a vivir sus últimos meses con gran intensidad. Sé que usted lo apreciaba mucho y se preocupaba por su salud. Y creo que los dos estaremos de acuerdo en que "murió con las botas puestas", como él quería.

BESARABIA

La escuela primaria en Yawo, una aldea insignificante, contaba una sola maestra y muy pocos alumnos. Fanny había comenzado el colegio a los seis años. Como hablaba yidish con su familia, se quejaba de tener pocos amigos, ya que los otros chicos eran rusos o rumanos y no querían jugar con ella. Muchos en el pueblito del *shtetl* estudiaban en casa o en la pequeña sinagoga con el rabino o el cantor. Los Radovitsky eran pobres, pero ilustrados, hablaban también francés, y quisieron que su hija aprendiera ruso en la escuelita para un día poder trabajar en una ciudad más grande.

Sentada bajo una higuera en el patio de la escuela, Fanny hacía pucheros y se apretaba la barriga con las manos. Era casi mediodía y esperaba ansiosa la única comida del día, aunque no fuera de su gusto. Temía que le dieran esa horrible *mămăligă*, una masa de harina de maíz, que desde hacía unos años preparaban los paisanos. Solo la toleraba mezclada con queso y crema agria, un plato que los rumanos llamaban *mămăligă cu brânză și smântână*. Su abuelita amaba esa crema, pronunciada *shmetene* en yidish, y se la agregaba a todo: a los pepinos en salmuera, a los arenques (cuando había), a los *vareniki* rellenos con queso y cebolla y especialmente a los *latkes*, las croquetas de papa favoritas de Fanny. Pero la niña aceptó sin protestar el almuerzo gratis de la escuela.

Había terminado apenas su porción cuando vio aparecer corriendo, desde la entrada, a su primo Simón, un jovencito de doce años, serio y determinado, muy adulto para su edad, que la levantó, gritándole con alarma:

—Vamos, Fanny. Me mandaron para llevarte ya mismo a casa, porque yo corro más rápido que tu mamá.

—Pero ¿por qué?

—Porque hay peligro en el pueblo y tenemos que escondernos. Pronto, pronto, que nos esperan...

Sin siquiera dar explicaciones a la maestra, Simón la arrastró de un brazo y la obligó a correr juntos por las calles de tierra.

La madre de Fanny ya los esperaba afuera con una valijita con ropa, un pan negro y un trozo de queso.

—Fanny, no te asustes, pero vamos a quedarnos por unos días en la granja del tío David. No hay tiempo que perder. En Yawo aún no ha pasado nada, pero cuentan que hay numerosos disturbios en Kishinev, en donde viven muchos judíos.

Allí mismo la montaron a un carro con otra gente y los dos caballos partieron al trote por el sendero rural, hacia el bosque que divisaban a lo lejos. Los adultos hablaban en voz baja de cosas que ella no entendía, pero que la aterrorizaban.

En el campo nadie los molestó. Cuando pudieron volver a Yawo les contaron que en ese mismo día de febrero de 1903 en que Simón la había rescatado en la escuelita, había ocurrido un trágico pogromo en Kishinev. En ese primer día de Pascua, una muchedumbre, dirigida por algunos curas y los cosacos del zar a caballo, atacó con sus sables a gente por las calles e incendió más de seiscientas casas con impunidad. Los sobrevivientes que podían se iban a Palestina o a la lejana América, donde otros judíos organizaban una asistencia financiera masiva para ayudarlos a emigrar.

Fanny fue creciendo en la pequeña aldea, pero veía cada vez menos a su primo. Decían que Simón se había juntado con anarquistas para proteger a obreros y campesinos víctimas del maltrato de los rusos. En 1905 había colaborado en la rebelión de los trabajadores, que anunciaba la futura Revolución rusa, y había combatido junto a la tripulación del acorazado Potemkin. Los marinos se habían amotinado contra el régimen brutal y tiránico de sus oficiales. La gota que rebasó el vaso fue cuando quisieron obligar a los marinos a comer un borsht con carne infestada por gusanos. Los rebeldes mataron a varios superiores, tomaron el control del barco y se dirigieron hacia Odesa. Cuando el ejército consiguió rodear el puerto y el navío, los rebeldes decidieron bombardear el famoso teatro, donde se reunía la plana mayor. Simón peleaba muy cerca, en las escaleras que bajaban hacia el puerto en el mar Negro, cuando los marinos atacaron. Si bien el puerto fue casi destruido, tanto él como el teatro sobrevivieron al ataque.

Un día de 1908, Simón, perseguido por las autoridades rusas, pasó a escondidas a despedirse de Fanny antes de subir a bordo de un carguero hacia el exilio en la Argentina. Ni ella ni Simón podían imaginar que esa sería la última vez que volverían a encontrarse.

Buenos Aires, 1913-1980

Luego del gran pogromo de Kishinev y de otros menores, la persecución antisemita se hizo frecuente y, por varios años, la vida de Fanny se redujo a las tareas domésticas y a aprender a cocinar con su abuelita, quien lo consideraba importante para conseguir un marido educado y trabajador. Aprendió a escribir en su casa, pero ya no volvió a la escuela del pueblo ni a estudiar ruso, y nunca llegó a hablarlo con fluidez.

De Simón no había noticias frescas, solo rumores de que continuaba su vida política en Argentina y, eventualmente, dejaron de recibir mensajes. En 1913, cuando la situación para los judíos de Besarabia se hacía intolerable, sus padres la embarcaron sola para que se uniera al tío David, ya exilado en Buenos Aires, donde trabajaba como sastre.

Cuando mi abuela Fanny llegó a su nueva patria, que imaginaba como un país exótico y remoto, la esperaban en el puerto su tío David con los hijos, pero se decepcionó al no ver a Simón.

—Tío David — preguntó alarmada—, ¿por qué no vino Simón a esperarme?

El tío tardó un rato en responder, como reflexionando con tristeza sobre lo que podía contarle:

—Mirá, Fanny, tu primo Simón no pudo venir al puerto porque está preso desde 1909 en una cárcel muy lejana en Ushuaia, en el sur de la Argentina, y no podemos visitarlo.

—Pero, tío, ¿por qué?, ¿qué le pasó? —preguntó, llorando desconsolada.

—Simón era anarquista en Rusia, y desde que llegó a este país encontró pobreza y vio que el Gobierno y la policía maltrataban a los trabajadores, igual que los cosacos de allá. Pronto se conectó con los anarquistas locales y comenzó a organizar huelgas y manifestaciones en el centro. Finalmente lo metieron preso y fue condenado a muchos años de cárcel.

—Pero ¿qué hizo para que lo mandaran tan lejos?

—Fanny, nosotros no sabemos qué pasó. Era muy joven, solo tenía dieciocho años, y aun así lo enviaron a Ushuaia, como a otros prisioneros peligrosos. Creemos que él no es culpable, son cargos falsos, pero no podemos ayudarlo. Mejor no hablar de eso con la gente, ya tenemos bastantes dificultades siendo judíos refugiados, y acá también hay antisemitas. Mejor no ponerse en evidencia.

Nunca más pronunciaron el nombre de Simón, ni en público ni entrecasa, por casi dos generaciones. Yo nunca supe de su existencia hasta 1978, cuando descubrí inesperadamente los detalles de este dramático episodio.

De Fanny, a quien llamábamos Lita, recuerdo su calidez maternal y su capacidad para relacionarse con la gente gracias a sus habilidades culinarias, ya que cocinaba con amor y maestría. Era muy poco conversadora y aprendió el español como para defenderse. De chico me enseñó algunas palabras en yidish, lengua con la que se comunicaba con su marido, Lito, y con sus tres hijas, pero nunca pude sonsacar información sobre su vida antes de llegar a la Argentina.

—Lita —le pregunté un día—, ¿no me hablarías un poco en ruso? Solo algunas palabras para escuchar cómo suena.

—El ruso no me gusta. No me acuerdo —dijo, después de una larga pausa, mirándome como recelosa de mis pedidos indiscretos.

—Pero ¿cómo puede ser que no te acuerdes, si vivías allí? —insistí descaradamente.

—Porque en Besarabia pasaban cosas feas, había pogromos y estábamos siempre escondidos.

Después de eso ya nunca más tocamos el asunto y tuve que recurrir a mi padre y a la enciclopedia para saber de qué estaba hablando. Parecía un velo que ella no podía quitarse, como si hubiese relegado al inconsciente toda su vida pasada. En cambio, nunca se olvidó de sus artes culinarias, y hasta las perfeccionó, en particular, las especialidades de su madre. Era generosa y aceptaba pedidos y sugerencias. Durante mi residencia en Medicina, solía llamarla por teléfono para invitarme a mí mismo a almorzar en su casa, que era mi refugio contra la comida desabrida del hospital. Uno de mis platos favoritos eran los *prakes*, las hojas de repollo rellenas con carne picada y especias, con una salsa de tomate y cebollas. Para mi sorpresa, otra gente no las conocía por ese nombre, a menos que fuesen judíos de un *shtetl* del sur de Rumanía, porque en Ucrania las llaman *halupki*, y en Rusia son *golubtsy*, a veces con mezcla de carne de vaca y de cerdo.

De chicos, visitábamos a veces con mis abuelos a otros exilados del *shtetl* de Besarabia. En un conventillo del barrio había una familia muy poco instruida, con tres hijos ya grandes: Asher, el más avanzado intelectualmente, era fabricante de artículos de cuero, billeteras, carteras de mujer y guantes. Motl era *cuéntenic*, un vendedor a domicilio de artículos generales y ropas (a pagar en cuotas mensuales, que escribía a mano en un cuaderno y controlaba los pagos escrupulosamente); y Velvl (o Vélvele), el más joven, tenía un déficit neurológico y cognitivo severo que nunca fue tratado. Vélvele imaginaba llevar un reloj en su muñeca derecha y podía decir la hora cuando, con gran crueldad, se la pedíamos para divertirnos. Ignorábamos nuestros propios defectos y la inmoralidad de esa conducta. Pero pagábamos esa deuda moral cuando jugábamos solos en el patio, en donde nos aterrorizaba un viejo algo demente, sentado a menudo bajo una higuera. El maniático sabía cómo darse vuelta los párpados de arriba usando un mondadientes, y mostraba la mucosa rojiza y lagrimosa para asustar a los chicos cuando nuestros padres o abuelos no estaban cerca.

Los sábados por la noche, un hermano de mi abuela emigrado de Odesa solía venir con otros amigos para jugar al póker, con un fondo muy alegre de música klezmer en discos de 78 rpm. Durante unas partidas fenomenales, se deleitaban con ensaladas de tomate, arenque, cebolla y *shmetene*, la infaltable crema agria. Me encantaba ir a comprarla a la oscurísima y diminuta tienda de un judío ruso en la calle Boedo, quien sacaba la crema con cucharones de unos enormes barriles. Yo heredé el gusto por esos manjares y por la música de Aarón Lebedeff, uno de los cantores en yidish tradicionales de Besarabia. Pero ahora constato que nunca en bastantes años escuché a la familia o a amigos mencionar la existencia del primo Simón, ni su encarcelamiento en una prisión muy lejana.

En 1978, en un vuelo a Buenos Aires, leí por primera vez En la Patagonia, que Bruce Chatwin publicara recientemente. Este apasionante relato de sus aventuras por el extremo sur de la Argentina, hasta Ushuaia y luego Punta Arenas, en la vecina Chile, me hizo recordar mis viajes de estudiante por la Patagonia. Visitábamos regiones poco frecuentadas, excepto por otros jóvenes mochileros, con poco dinero y sin buenos equipos para explorar. Nuestras inversiones más costosas eran las botas de cuero y las bolsas de dormir hechas a mano, con plumón o duvet que escapaba por todas las costuras. Teníamos poco abrigo, casi ninguna ropa impermeable, y pasábamos frío bastante a menudo. Íbamos a pie, con mapas insuficientes y por picadas mal señalizadas, para acampar al borde de algún lago azul. Nuestro sueño era llegar un día hasta la mítica ciudad de Ushuaia, un sitio inalcanzable por lo remoto y por nuestra falta de recursos. En cambio, nos conformamos con alcanzar Esquel, en la provincia de Chubut, fundada por galeses en 1895. Tuvimos el gusto de viajar en La Trochita, el minúsculo tren de trocha angosta, que hoy llaman *The Old Patagonian Express*, debido al libro de Paul Theroux.

Un día en Esquel conocimos a un mayor de la aviación que se interesó por charlar con nosotros, estudiantes de Medicina. Decía tener "afinidad por los médicos" y que su hígado estaba debilitado (seguramente por la bebida). Tenía que volar por la mañana en un avión militar hasta Ushuaia y le rogamos que nos permitiera acompañarlo. Para nuestra gran sorpresa, aceptó. Nos presentamos con mucha ilusión a las 4 de la madrugada en el aeropuerto. El mayor apareció como a las 5, rodeado por una gran comitiva de señoras y niños con numerosas valijas. Allí nos enteramos de que, como venía su familia, el vuelo estaba lleno, y que "lo lamentaba mucho". Mi deseo de visitar esa ciudad utópica quedó en suspenso por cantidad de años.

Chatwin describía en su libro a varios personajes inusitados, como Butch Cassidy y el Sundance Kid, asaltantes de bancos y de trenes, y otros revolucionarios y anarquistas refugiados que dieron color a esa región. Entre ellos mencionaba la vida heroica y azarosa de un tal Simón Radovitzky, un prisionero célebre en la colonia penal en Ushuaia. En 1908, durante una huelga y marcha por el barrio norte de Buenos Aires, este Radovitzky había matado con una bomba al temible jefe de policía, el coronel Falcón.

Apenas llegado a la Argentina, me precipité a interrogar a mi madre sobre el nombre del prisionero. Con gran reticencia y luego de un largo silencio, me confirmó que se trataba de Simón, el olvidado primo de mi ya fallecida abuela Fanny. Yo había descubierto fortuitamente su existencia, y las terribles razones de su encarcelamiento, el prolongado secreto de nuestra familia. Desde ese día, mi curiosidad sobre Simón se complementó con mi sueño de visitar Ushuaia, hasta transformarse en una obsesión, que solo pude satisfacer muchos años más tarde, siendo ya un profesional bien establecido en Estados Unidos.

Ushuaia, 2001 a la actualidad

El avión estaba fresco y nuestras ligeras ropas eran solo apropiadas para el veranito de diciembre en Buenos Aires. Pasada la turbulencia sobre la Patagonia, descendimos rápidamente hacia nuestra meta juvenil: la legendaria Ushuaia, en Tierra del Fuego. Aterrizamos a unos 100 m de la terminal y, sin túnel, bajamos por la escalerita. La ciudad que imaginábamos soleada y cálida nos recibió con vientos de 70 km por hora sobre la pista y una inesperada nevada que nos dejó casi blancos al entrar al aeropuerto. Esta helada introducción nos hizo pensar en el calvario que debió sufrir Simón en el presidio austral. La ciudad se sitúa en el extremo sur de la isla de Tierra del Fuego, en el confín de Sudamérica, apenas separada de la Antártida por 600 km de mar. La gente de allí la consideraba como el "fin del mundo", y una bodega local se había apropiado de ese nombre para sus vinos. Por debajo del paralelo 42, era —y aún es— puerto libre de impuestos a la importación. Paradójicamente, muchos beneficiarios de tal "libertad" ignoran la época trágica y sufrida en que aún estaba habilitada la colonia penal.

Por la mañana, las casas bajas de colores, frente al mar extremadamente azul y violento, con un marco de montañas nevadas, nos recordaron a Juneau, en Alaska, en las antípodas de Norteamérica. Mientras nuestros amigos gozaban de un movido crucero por los canales fueguinos, mi esposa, Diana, y yo nos dirigimos al Museo del Fin del Mundo para investigar sobre mi pariente y sus desventuras. El edificio era pequeño y en la sala principal una maestra contaba la historia de la ciudad a un grupo de escolares de la primaria, que parecían fascinados por el relato. Terminada la charla, nos presentamos.

—Señorita, perdone si nos quedamos a escucharla sin permiso, pero nos encantó su clase.

—Por supuesto, señor, los turistas son siempre bienvenidos. Tenemos tanto para contarles a los niños sobre una larga historia: los yaganes y los onas, nuestros pueblos indígenas y nuestros orígenes ingleses, como la familia de Thomas Bridges, y la travesía de Darwin en el Beagle. Como sabrán, bordeamos el canal del mismo nombre.

—En realidad, si bien somos turistas, tenemos un interés especial en la historia de la colonia penal. Un primo de mi abuela, se llamaba Simón Radovitzky, fue prisionero durante años. ¿Podríamos ver algunos documentos de la época?

—¡No me diga! Su pariente era un prisionero muy notorio, pero me sorprende verlos. No recuerdo que sus familiares hayan venido a informarse. Solo pasaron por aquí algunos historiadores o anarquistas como él. Vengan conmigo, puedo mostrarles fotos y documentos.

La maestra y directora del museo nos hizo entrar a una sala más pequeña, con la biblioteca y el archivo. La pared estaba cubierta por fotos históricas y se detuvo frente al retrato de un hombre bastante delgado, lampiño, pero con un fino bigotito bajo su nariz aguileña y una cara curiosamente triangular. Se veía malnutrido, pero con una actitud desafiante.

—Este era Radovitzky, uno de los prisioneros más célebres. Estuvo preso más de veinte años hasta que lo liberaron y creo que se fue a España y acabó peleando en la Guerra Civil.

Nos miró con curiosidad, quizá buscando algún parecido conmigo, o analizando mis emociones, y ofreció enseñarnos otras fotos históricas. Era mi primera ocasión de conocer detalles sobre Simón, a quien nuestra familia había relegado al olvido. Se infiltraba un viento frígido por una de las ventanas entreabiertas. De pronto me sentí muy lejos de casa, en el "último confín de la Tierra", como lo había descrito Lucas Bridges en su libro *Uttermost Part of the Earth*. Simón debió imaginarse en las antípodas de Besarabia, su región natal, casi en otro planeta. Solo encontraría símiles entre la brutalidad de los guardias en el penal con los cosacos del zar en su juventud.

—Les puedo decir que este hombre era muy querido por los prisioneros, que lo habían apodado "el ángel de Ushuaia" —aclaró la maestra—. Lo admiraban por su fuerza interior y por resistir a las torturas interminables a que lo sometía el director de la prisión. Reconocían su humanidad y su resistencia a las dictaduras, lo que mitigaba que hubiese asesinado a Falcón. Finalmente, un movimiento popular de apoyo en la capital logró que lo liberaran después de veintiún años de prisión. Este detalle puede interesarle —prosiguió—, es una foto del MV Monte Cervantes, un barco que naufragó frente a Ushuaia en los años veinte. Algunos prisioneros del penal, incluso Radovitzky, fueron obligados a rescatar a los náufragos.

—¡Qué coincidencia! —intervino Diana de pronto—. Aída, una vieja amiga de mi madre, fue pasajera en el Cervantes y una de las sobrevivientes del naufragio. ¿No la habrá rescatado Simón, así como ayudó a esconderse a tu abuelita Fanny?

Si bien mi familia ignoró la existencia de Simón, quedan anarquistas que aún intentan emularlo. Hace dos años, durante una visita a Buenos Aires, nos alojamos en un hotel a doscientos metros de la Recoleta, el cementerio más famoso de la ciudad, donde reposan los restos de familias aristocráticas y de ciudadanos ilustres, entre ellos, el coronel Falcón. Curiosamente, también su tumba queda a la misma distancia de Callao y Quintana, la esquina en que había sido asesinado. Cuando nos disponíamos a tomar una siestita, una fuerte explosión afuera sacudió el hotel. Al despertarnos todo seguía en calma y encendimos la televisión para ver las noticias. Lo primero que relató el locutor fue algo sorprendente:

"Último momento —dijo casi sonriendo—: En el cementerio de la Recoleta, hace dos horas, una pareja de anarquistas intentó explotar una bomba frente a la tumba del coronel Falcón, en el aniversario de su muerte. Ingresaron al cementerio casi a la hora del cierre, uno de ellos disfrazado de mujer con una peluca rubia, en una silla de ruedas, y el otro empujándola con amabilidad. Al llegar a la tumba de Falcón, el que venía vestido de mujer preparó la bomba, pero antes quiso tomarse un selfie como recuerdo. La bomba detonó accidentalmente en ese mismo instante, amputándole una mano y casi la mitad de la cara. La policía está investigando posibles contactos con otros grupos de anarquistas".

Nos sentamos en la cama, con la boca abierta, frente al hecho tan improbable de que coincidiendo con nuestra visita, unos imitadores modernos quisieran repetir la conducta de mi pariente cien años más tarde.

Ni la prensa ni los anarquistas supieron que,

formando un triángulo equilátero entre la tumba de Falcón, con la esquina del asesinato en 1908 y con el hotel, en ese instante de la explosión fallida se hallaban posiblemente los únicos, o los últimos, familiares en la Argentina de Simón Radovitsky.

SEATTLE, 2020

Hace pocas semanas, buscando información en Internet sobre este relato, encontré de manera azarosa que en 2016 un escritor argentino había publicado un libro ilustrado sobre El prisionero 155, subtitulado Simón Radovitzky. No era la primera vez que daba con información esencial sobre el tema de uno de mis cuentos y ficciones, pero este descubrimiento me tocó muy fuertemente. De inmediato pensé en mi madre y en mi abuela, que fallecieron sin enterarse de este episodio trágico de nuestro antepasado de Besarabia.

No tardé en tener el libro en mis manos. Estaba ilustrado de forma exquisita por un gran dibujante y narrador, Agustín Comotto, ahora radicado en Cataluña. El texto contenía firmes referencias históricas de varios archivos y contactos valiosos con un historiador amigo personal de Radovitzky. Pocos días más tarde hablábamos por WhatsApp con Agustín, tan maravillado como yo de encontrar a un descendiente cercano del sujeto de su biografía. Para mi sorpresa, me reveló que otros familiares, desconocidos para mí, habían emigrado a Estados Unidos, pero cambiando su apellido, quizá para evitar referencias a nuestro pariente común. No así otra prima hermana de Simón, Emilia Radovitzky, que yo nunca había escuchado mencionar. Ella no temía declarar su relación directa con él, y aseguraba estar "orgullosa de que hubiese matado a un homicida".

La existencia de mis antepasados en Besarabia y la aparición de nuevos personajes relacionados siguen afectándome en un ciclo interminable. Desde el punto de vista del hinduismo, la vida es eterna, aparece y desaparece como "las olas y las burbujas en la corriente del tiempo", según me había explicado con paciencia el doctor Nair, mi tutor en Trivandrum. Hace poco, durante unos arreglos en nuestra casa de Mercer Island, conocimos a un carpintero experto y silencioso, como de unos cincuenta años. Era un emigrante de Europa del Este que había llegado hacia solo siete años a los Estados Unidos. Nunca supe si estaba o no documentado, aunque eso no es importante. Era el primer obrero en aparecer temprano por la mañana, y a los pocos instantes estaba ya enfrascado en sus tareas. Con un joven asistente, que resultó ser su yerno, hablaban en un idioma que pensé sería ruso o ucraniano.

Según mi costumbre, al tomar el desayuno, yo le ofrecía compartir conmigo un capuchino de buena calidad, con granos tostados en el Véneto, al norte de Italia. Su agradecimiento era palpable, parecía sorprendido por lo inesperado del gesto, y con una sonrisa tímida lo bebía con lentitud y gusto, para recomenzar de inmediato su trabajo de carpintería, y con más dedicación aún.

—Muy buen café —comentó el primer día, con admiración y una sacudida vertical de la cabeza.

En una de estas ocasiones, aproveché para preguntarle algo que ya sospechaba:

—Elijah, ¿de qué país viene? ¿Es de Rumanía, como su jefe? Escuché que hablaba en otro idioma con su ayudante. ¿Por qué dicen da, igual que en ruso?

No esperaba una respuesta muy compleja, porque su inglés era rudimentario.

—No, vengo de Besarabia, hoy parte de Moldavia. Mi yerno es ucraniano, y yo puedo hablar su idioma, y también, ruso y rumano.

Mi asombro fue enorme al escuchar nuevamente el nombre de esa región, la que yo imaginaba desaparecida, o integrada con los países limítrofes.

—Elijah —le respondí, un poco emocionado—, mi familia también salió de Besarabia, de donde escapó mi abuelita para ir a la Argentina. Ella era de Yawo, una aldea muy pequeña, no creo que la conozca. También los abuelos de mi esposa vienen de Kishinev y de Akkerman, que eran ciudades más grandes.

Lo sorprendí tanto que suspendió su trabajo por unos segundos.

—¡Claro que conozco Chişinau, que llamaban Kishinev en yidish; ¡también mi hermano vive en Akkerman, pero ahora le decimos Belgorod-Dnestrovskyy!

Su entusiasmo era llamativo, casi como el mío al reconocernos como iguales. Desde ese momento, demostró aún mayor dedicación y orgullo profesional, con un deseo de satisfacer especialmente a su nuevo cliente. Cuando le pedí que arreglara las patas rotas de un escritorio de Diana, el resultado fue espectacular, de gran calidad, y quedó mejor que nuevo. Intenté ofrecerle una propina, pero tardó en aceptar, y me dijo algo curioso:

—Propina no necesario, usted especial, como hermano. Usted da buen café por la mañana. Es bendición para mí y yo quiero bendición para usted, God bless —agregó, expresión seguramente aprendida de los protestantes de aquí.

—Elijah, qué nombre interesante, muy religioso. Nosotros lo llamaríamos "Eliahu" en hebreo.

—Yes! Eliahu es nombre bíblico, un profeta. Mi apellido es M..., podría ser... no estoy seguro.

Nuevamente sonrió con timidez, como si el tema fuera bien conocido para él. Pensé que su apellido era decididamente de origen judío, aunque *God bless* sugería más bien que fuese cristiano como su yerno. Podría especular que su familia judía en Besarabia debió convertirse al cristianismo años atrás, para sobrevivir al antisemitismo y a las cíclicas persecuciones por los rusos, o los rumanos, ucranianos y por los alemanes en la Segunda Guerra Mundial.

Al terminar el trabajo, un viernes al atardecer, Elijah vino a despedirse y me entregó formalmente un papelito con su nombre y dirección, teléfono y la consabida frase, ahora manuscrita: *¡God bless!* Los dos usábamos máscara para protegernos del covid-19, pero le di un caluroso apretón de manos, ignorando la recomendada distancia social. Mi flamante amigo, con una gran sonrisa y un cierto orgullo, me deseó con claridad en hebreo, inesperadamente:

¡Shabát Shalom!

Acknowledgments

This book owes its existence to the unconditional support, alertness of spirit, and literary vision of Diana, my wife and lifelong companion. She was the first to read these tales and to offer her honest and insightful opinion. Many of the stories in this volume are a testament to our many years of shared history.

As a bilingual job, it required the expert attention of two dedicated language consultants: Stephanie Lawyer in English, and Lupe Rodríguez Santizo in Spanish.

My sincere thanks to all of them.

Agradecimientos

Este libro debe su existencia al apoyo incondicional, el espíritu alerta, y la visión literaria de Diana, mi esposa de siempre, la primera persona en leer estos cuentos y en ofrecer su opinión crítica y honesta. Nuestras historias se entrelazan y multiplican con los años hasta cuajar en este volumen de muchos episodios compartidos.

Como trabajo bilingüe, exigió la atención experta de dos dedicadas consultoras lingüísticas: Stephanie Lawyer en inglés y Lupe Rodríguez Santizo en español.

A todas ellas, mi sincero agradecimiento.